A PRACTICAL GUIDE TO EQUAL OPPORTUNITIES, 2ND EDITION

Hyacinth Malik

Published in 2003 by:
Nelson Thornes Ltd
Delta Place
27 Bath Road
CHELTENHAM
GL53 7TH
United Kingdom

03 04 05 06 07 / 10 9 8 7 6 5 4 3 2 1

A catalogue record for this book is available from the British Library

ISBN 0 7487 7079 8

Illustrations by Jane Bottomley
Page make-up by Northern Phototypesetting Co. Ltd, Bolton

Printed and bound in Spain by GraphyCems

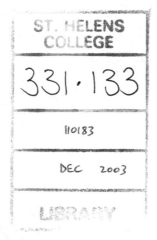

CONTENTS

INTRODUCTION

This book will not provide all the answers to issues surrounding anti-bias, anti-discrimination and equal opportunities. It is a highly practical guide, covering the important issues of race, gender and disability in a straight-forward and student-friendly way. Its aim is to develop knowledge, understanding and skills in practising and promoting equality of opportunity – not just with children, but also with nursery staff, with parents and with the community at large.

The key to the book is that all children and their families are **different, but equal**, and it is with this philosophy in mind that the book explores equal opportunities issues with its readers. It proposes that, together, we all make a difference. It encourages a proactive, hands-on approach and emphasises good practice in all aspects of working with children and their families. The book features regular activities and case studies. It keeps the reader updated and informed about present issues.

A Practical Guide to Equal Opportunities, 2nd edition encourages its readers to take the first step on a long journey towards providing a whole-team approach to equal opportunities. The responsibility for equal opportunities education is never in the hands of a single individual. If it were, we would all be guilty of devaluing equality for all children and their families. All children need to feel equally valued and the rights of a child are paramount.

This book is written to continue to enrich all our lives.

ACKNOWLEDGEMENTS

The author would like to thank her beloved daughter and best friend, Nazneen Malik, for all her support and the interest she has taken in the compilation of the 2nd edition of this book, and extends her respect to all those who continue to contribute to high standards and practices in equality, anti-bias and anti-discrimination in all settings.

The author and publishers are grateful to the following for supplying photographs: Asco Educational Suppliers Ltd (p. 147); James Galt & Co. Limited (p. 148).

1 AN INTRODUCTION TO EQUAL OPPORTUNITIES

This chapter covers:
- **What are equal opportunities?**
- **Equality**
- **Stereotyping**
- **Prejudice**
- **Discrimination**
- **Harassment**
- **'The differences between us'**
- **The importance of equal opportunities**

What are equal opportunities?

There can be no quality in early childhood services unless there is **equality of opportunity.**

Equality of opportunity means:
- providing open access to early childhood services to allow *every* child and family to participate fully
- treating *all* children equally, based on their individual needs.

Lack of access leads to poor self-esteem, lack of confidence, misunderstandings, lack of respect, **stereotyping** and **discrimination**, with damaging consequences for children.

No one in society should suffer discrimination because of his or her **race**, **gender**, class, culture, age, religion, **disability** or sexual orientation. This is an important point for people working with young children to remember. The younger the child, the less likely he or she is to challenge and confront prejudice and discrimination. It is a child's right under the 1989 Children Act to have all his or her needs met, regardless of their age, race, **sex**, disability or religion.

KEY POINTS

- Race – a label that is socially constructed, it describes a group of people who see themselves, or who are seen by others, to have the same ethnic origin. It is often an assumption based on a person's outward appearance and skin colour.

- Gender – a label that is socially constructed, it describes the cultural and psychological expectations of behaviour as being either typically male behaviour or typically female behaviour. It is a product of socialisation. Dress is also a part of this.
- Disability – this refers to differences in physical or mental ability or sensory impairment. People make assumptions about disability and make negative judgements about those who are seen as disabled.
- Sex – a biological term, it refers to the biological differences between males and females. Sex is usually unchanging, but can be changed by surgery.

Equal rights legislation (covered in Chapter 2), which governs equal opportunities, tries to ensure that people are treated equally on the basis of individual needs. However, legislation on its own cannot guarantee this, and people do still experience unfairness and inequality in areas such as education, employment, housing, training and health care. Equal opportunity allows an individual to reach his or her full potential and it is a constitutional right.

During your training, you will meet children with different disabilities, languages, cultures, religions, lifestyles, skin colours, dress and backgrounds, and with different behaviours. This rich variety demands that you should have a professional attitude, one that is grounded in equal rights practices.

This college practises equal opportunities: Janet is able to use the computer to wordprocess her assignment – the computer facilities have been designed so that her wheelchair fits easily under the desk.

Equality

Social inequalities are present in all societies in one form or another, influencing every aspect of people's lives and attitudes. From an early age, children are influenced by examples of sexist, racist, disablist, and classist behaviours, images, attitudes and languages that they hear and see around them.

The consequences for black and for white children, for girls and for boys, and for children with disabilities are different. But *all* children are at risk of inequality, and intervention is necessary to promote equality and to provide equal chances for all children.

Equality means:

- valuing a diverse, multicultural, multilingual and multiracial society
- valuing individuals' genders, disabilities, cultures, religions and lifestyles
- offering and providing equal chances to everyone in society, irrespective of variation within the population
- not endorsing the concept of superiority and inferiority within and among the population
- maintaining and upholding each individual's human right not to be discriminated against and denied his or her equality
- recognising that there is a variety of child-rearing practices which are all equally effective in providing security for children, and that children and their families should be viewed as unique and individual

Children should be encouraged to achieve their full potential without discriminating barriers, such as sex stereotyping, which lead to disadvantage.

- actively opposing negative discrimination and encouraging a positive world view of people, promoting positive images of boys and girls, black, white and disabled children, of all cultures, religions and languages, valuing diversity as equal
- having an equitable society, with everyone receiving equal treatment under the law.

Equality is a right, not a privilege – children should achieve their full potential without discriminating barriers, which lead to disadvantage and which deny them their legitimate and legal rights.

Activity

In a group:

a) Make a list of points that identify what the term 'equality' means to you.
b) From the list, identify what you think are the four most important points and the four least important points.
c) Keeping these in your mind, try to agree on eight key statements that you all agree are a reflection of your understanding of the term 'equality'.
d) Discuss the reasons for your choices.

GOOD PRACTICE

- Evaluate books and resources that you use in your placement, ensuring that they reflect equality.
- Confront practices of inequality.
- Advise new staff, visitors and parents on the promotion of equality.

SOCIALISATION

Socialisation is the process of learning the norms, values and expectations of the society in which you live, including language, gender behaviour, culture and religion.

The socialisation process begins when a child is born and continues throughout his or her life. During the early years the child learns many of the basic behaviour patterns of society. This is **primary socialisation**, probably the most important part of the process. In most societies, the family takes the main responsibility for this, building the foundations of the child's knowledge. As the child moves into the wider society, **secondary socialisation** takes place, when he or she begins to learn from a

For young children, much socialisation occurs during play.

wider range of people, media and institutions, such as nurseries, play-groups, childminders and schools.

Observation of gender-related performances in young children is supported by researchers such as Smith and Daglish (1977). They found that boys between the ages of one and two usually prefer cars and lorries, whereas girls of the same age prefer to play with soft toys and dolls. Infants have no innate (inherited) gender behaviour, but learn this quickly through selective reinforcement and gender role models. The researchers suggest that it is likely that, unconsciously, parents and others communicate a wealth of information regarding gender-appropriate behaviour to infants, in their efforts to socialise them.

Infants also learn from attitudes expressed by others – research by Milner (1973) and Maxime (1983) indicates that children as young as three years old are aware of differences of race.

GOOD PRACTICE

- Avoid negative examples of gender roles.
- Treat boys and girls equally.
- Be aware of the way in which language can be used to reinforce gender stereotypes.

KEY POINTS

- Primary socialisation usually occurs in the home with family and close friends.

Male nursery nurses Darren and Samuel are positive role models.

● Secondary socialisation includes other agencies, such as playgroups, childminders, schools, etc.

Stereotyping

Stereotyping is the over-generalised way of labelling people long before we really know them. It is an assumption based on inaccurate, preconceived ideas and misinformation. It denies people the opportunity of meeting and interacting as individuals, and as a consequence we can misjudge each other.

Activity
Think about a holiday you have had and share this with your colleagues. Working in a group, discuss the following questions and issues.
a) Before the holiday:
  ● Did you have any fears or anxieties about the holiday?
  ● What did you know about the culture, food, language, place and the people?
  ● What were your perceptions about the people? Would you like them?
  ● What thoughts did you have about the place you were going to visit? Record the group's answers, and reflect on how your negative thoughts and ideas changed during the holiday, from feelings of anxiety and fear to feelings of like and enjoyment.

b) After the holiday:
- Make a list of things you liked about the holiday.
- What negative thoughts did you have about the people that changed to positive ones?
- What did you learn and enjoy about the language, culture and the country?
- How did your negative preconceptions about the holiday prove to be wrong?
- List the things about the holiday that made you happy and would make you go again.

c) Having compared your experiences before and after the holiday, identify the following from your list:
- Stereotyping that caused you to discriminate negatively.
- Experiences that enriched your learning and changed your negative stereotyping.
- How information you had before the holiday caused you to be prejudicial about the people, food, language, culture or lifestyle.

d) Design a display for a group of children in a reception class based on your happy holiday. The aim of your display is to share your positive experiences with the children. The display should focus on the holiday, the people, the language spoken, the culture and lifestyle, food and religion. Include anything your feel would aid the children's learning about the place you visited. You could use it as a story-telling session.
- Avoid using negative stereotypes in the display.
- Remember to make the display appropriate for the children's ages and stages of learning and development.

Use your holiday photos as part of your display about your happy holiday.

e) Evaluate how you have examined your own knowledge of equality practices and stereotyping in this activity.
How, in part (d) of this activity, did you participate in children's positive learning?

KEY POINTS

- Misperception is based on fear and anxiety.
- Negative stereotyping can be changed by being open to new experiences.

Most people have stereotypical views of one sort or another; labelling someone by the way they dress is a form of stereotyping. Attitudes towards others are often based on such stereotypes. However, researchers into stereotyping have found that very few stereotypes are actually true representations of individuals.

Stereotypes may be positive or negative. Inequality arises when **negative stereotypes** are used, because the people who use them are unable to see and value individual differences among people. Forming accurate perceptions of others is important in all social situations if we are to interact and communicate effectively and equally.

A lot of stereotyping happens in a child's environment – remarks are often made about expectations of young children long before they have an opportunity to show that they are different from the label ascribed to them.

This family is breaking a stereotype – Sabina is teaching her son, Anwar, to cook.

A mother caring for her daughters – why is this a negative gender role stereotype for the two girls?

You should be aware of negative images of groups of people in society based on race, gender, class and disability, and of how these are communicated to children. If young children are constantly bombarded with negative images of people, they will come to believe them to be true. If left unchallenged, a negative image becomes a **self-fulfilling prophecy**, especially if the image portrayed is significant to that child.

KEY POINT

A self-fulfilling prophecy is a process of conditioning people to behave in ways based on other people's expectations of them.

CASE STUDY

Zoe is disabled and is in the reception class at her local school. She is partially mobile and uses a wheelchair to get around. Zoe has a non-teaching assistant to assist when she needs help getting in and out of the wheelchair. She is very popular with the other children and joins them in their play activities at playtime.

Zoe is always frightened at story time because the reception class teacher pays her little attention and she is often referred to as the 'special needs girl' or 'the girl in the wheelchair'. Whenever the teacher speaks to Zoe she talks in 'baby language' and uses a high tone of voice compared to her normal tone with the other children. Zoe sees this as shouting and is unable to understand why the teacher communicates to her in this manner.

Because of this, Zoe feels misunderstood. She no longer asks questions at story time and is beginning to behave as if she does not understand the stories, when in fact she does. She is now communicating to the teacher with baby language, which is not how she communicates with her family at home. It all started at school.

1 Is the teacher negatively stereotyping Zoe? If so, how and why?
2 What is the teacher's perception of Zoe?
3 What is her expectation of Zoe's potential?
4 How is Zoe conforming to a self-fulfilling prophecy?
5 How will this affect Zoe's equality?
6 How could the teacher's attitude change positively to encourage Zoe to fulfil her potential?
7 How is this interaction influencing Zoe's self-perception?

STEREOTYPES

A **stereotype** is a type of 'schema'. Berkowitz (1986) defines a schema as 'a cognitive [i.e. in the mind] structure consisting of the perceiver's knowledge or beliefs about something'. A stereotype is, therefore, a mental structure which contains an individual's beliefs and knowledge about a particular topic.

Cohen, a social researcher, carried out an experiment in 1981 to investigate how stereotypes affect people's memory of facts about other people.

Those participating in the experiment were told that they were going to watch either a video showing a librarian or a video showing a waitress.

The video was specially designed so that the woman the people saw (who was eating and talking with her husband) possessed characteristics that were known to go with some of the stereotypes of both these occupations. For example, she wore glasses, played the piano, had been to Europe – stereotypical characteristics of a librarian; she also liked pop music and went bowling – stereotypical characteristics of a waitress.

When Cohen tested the participants' memory of the woman's characteristics, those who had been told she was a librarian tended to remember more stereotypical librarian characteristics. Those who had been told that she was a waitress remembered more stereotypical waitress characteristics, even though all the participants had seen the same video. Participants in this experiment remembered information that was consistent with the stereotype they had in mind and ignored information that was irrelevant.

Activity

In the research described above, everyone saw the same video of a woman talking to her husband.

a) What did the researcher do that caused those watching the video to give different answers?

b) What were the stereotypical characteristics of the waitress?

c) What were the stereotypical characteristics of the librarian?

d) How did these stereotypes influence the participants' memories of facts about the woman in the video? (Remember – before they watched the video, one group was told that the woman was a librarian, the other that she was a waitress.)

e) Why is stereotyping unreliable in this research?

Stereotyping does not necessarily have to be a 'bad thing', because it can be used as a way of summarising groups, and does have its uses. However, it becomes an issue when it is used negatively to devalue individuals and groups of people.

Stereotyping must be done carefully, if at all, and attention must be paid to all the information received about groups of people and individuals. It can be based on race, gender, social class, disability, occupation and even accent, and can be a dangerous source of bias in person perception, creating a false impression of others. Stereotypes can be resistant to change and result in **prejudice** against groups of people in society. For example, racism is resistant to change and results in black people being disadvantaged.

The consequences of such negative stereotyping are damaging to children's perception of themselves and others. Children who grow up feeling that they are inferior or who are told they are inferior by others because of their gender, disability, race, class, language, religion or culture are being deprived of the chance to achieve their full potential. On the other hand, children who are allowed to assume superiority because of their colour, gender, their physical abilities and class will have false perceptions of humanity.

Activity

a) Below is a list of words. Organise them under the following headings:
  - Girls/women
  - Boys/men
  - Either.

gentle	busy	dependent
feminine	kind	cheeky
warm	emotional	sensitive
boisterous	competitive	energetic
aggressive	helpful	

b) Discuss your list in groups.
c) How have you stereotyped?
d) What images did you use?
e) Where do the stereotypes come from?
f) Which did you positively and/or negatively stereotype?

GOOD PRACTICE

Never prejudge anyone based on preconceived ideas or stereotypical labels. Anti-bias and anti-discrimination should be paramount in your practices.

Prejudice

Prejudice literally means prejudgement, and results from a person's (or a group's) failure to explore alternative explanations or possibilities for their stereotypes. It can be positive or negative (i.e. in favour of, or against, people or things). Prejudiced attitudes often result in discrimination, which involves negative actions towards individuals or groups of people.

When we describe someone as being prejudiced, we mean that they hold certain attitudes and beliefs (stereotypes) about a person, group of people or a thing. This attitude is usually fixed in a way that the person is reluctant to change. When we talk of prejudice, we are usually referring to negative conditions and negative attitudes towards other people, such as:

- sexism – prejudice based on a person's biological sex
- racism – prejudice based on a person's race
- disablism – prejudice based on a person's disability.

Prejudice is learned through the process of socialisation. Children learn many of their attitudes and prejudices from their environment and from people around them. Some researchers suggest that children under the age of seven are cognitively immature (i.e. they are unable to understand what is going on, because they haven't enough knowledge) and therefore cannot avoid making judgements based on learned prejudices.

As they mature, children learn to make important differentiation in their stereotypes, and this is based on the availability of positive experiences. The child could be exposed to supportive stereotypes in the media, or in the family, or it could be that a certain parenting style predisposes a child to retain a prejudiced attitude towards other groups of people.

Any theory of behaviour that explains social issues such as prejudice entirely in terms of what *individuals* are like has limitations as an explanation of social prejudice. Evidence suggests that specific *groups of people* are identified as targets at different times, for example in cases of racial violence.

Prejudice is not always directed at the same group and different degrees of social prejudice exist among a variety of personality types. As society changes, prejudice changes. For example, during the twentieth century, the main focus of racism in the UK shifted from Jewish people to black people.

The culture of a society has considerable influence on individual prejudices, if one group in society has privileges and others are denied those privileges. Those who are privileged may feel defensive of their position, while those who are not may feel frustrated and disadvantaged.

A culture with a negative prejudice can have an effect on its population. For example, social researchers such as Rogers and Frantz found that in 1962 in Zimbabwe, white immigrants developed more anti-black attitudes the longer they stayed in the country. This suggests that their attitudes were adjusting to the racist white culture in which they found themselves.

THEORIES OF PREJUDICE

Several theories have been proposed in an attempt to explain prejudice:

- biological theory
- psychoanalytical theory
- cultural explanations.

Biological theory

Biological explanations of prejudice propose that human social behaviour is basically identical to that of animals and that xenophobia (fear of and hostility towards other people) is the result of a need to protect people who share the same gene. The discrimination practised by the Nazis against Jews in Germany during the Second World War might be put forward as an example of the biological theory.

The biological gene is used as a magical explanation of prejudice, but prejudice is usually regarded as a more complex social issue than just a product of simple causes. Rose *et al.* (1984), who are researchers in this field, point out that similarity is not 'homology', i.e. just because something looks similar, we cannot reliably conclude that it is the same thing. For example, an aggressive action by an animal is very different from an aggressive act by a human being, both in terms of its causes and its consequences to others.

Psychoanalytical theory

The psychoanalytical explanation of prejudice sees it as a result of deep-seated motives within the individual. This is known as the authoritarian personality proposal. It suggests that prejudice is present in people's personalities, that certain types of people are more inclined to be prejudiced than others and that it is the result of a strict and rigid upbringing.

Cultural explanations

A negative prejudice, which is deeply embedded in a culture, can lead to high levels of discrimination in that society. However, research in The Netherlands suggests that the reverse can be possible – that a culture with a positive attitude towards groups of people (as in the case of The Netherlands) can influence the levels of racial discrimination. The research found that, in The Netherlands, the occurrence of racial discrimination was lower than in the UK, which has a similar black and white population.

None of these theoretical explanations can justifiably explain the causes of prejudice. Nor can other explanations, such as **scapegoating** theory (which is used to explain prejudice in periods of economic decline or social tension, when certain groups of people experience discrimination), be used to explain issues that are more complex in a society.

KEY POINT

Scapegoating means to project the blame for something on to others, instead of looking at the real causes. For example, an individual who is frustrated with being unemployed might say 'I am unemployed because black people take all our jobs'. This is the scapegoating of black people (i.e. blaming black people for unemployment). The reality might really be that 'I am unemployed because I have no skills to offer the job market' or that 'recession increases economic decline, resulting in unemployment in certain industries'.

Activity
In groups, discuss these questions:
a) What is prejudice?
b) Is prejudice learned or inherited?
c) How could prejudice be reduced?

Some children and adults are more prejudiced than others. Researchers such as Wetherly in 1961 and Green and Berkowitz in 1967 suggest that tolerant sensitivity to children's frustration with authority will make prejudice less likely.

The general explanations offered above do not justify prejudicial behaviour towards others. If the causes of prejudice are found to be based in interpersonal interactions (interaction between people), then change may be possible. However, if the causes are seen as 'deeper', at the personality level, then changes will be much more difficult to achieve. Explanations of prejudice based on the authoritarian personality and biological

Prejudice can be reduced by encouraging contact between groups of people with equal status. This can begin in the nursery with children playing together, irrrespective of race and gender.

explanations suggest that prejudice is developed in the early years of life through childcare practices. If this is the case, then re-education in the early years is of paramount importance.

Theories explaining inter-group conflict as causes of prejudice are susceptible to change, since prejudice is seen as adopted and learned through conformity to groups, power or impact of the mass media. Prejudice could be reduced by encouraging contact between groups of people with equal status, thus changing negative stereotypes and leading to co-operation between individuals and to equality practices.

GOOD PRACTICE

- Always critically evaluate theories that justify prejudice and discrimination.
- None of the theories described above are based on good equal opportunity practices. To use any of them would be to disadvantage children.
- Prejudice can be reduced and changed by people using equal opportunities approaches and practices.
- Always challenge these theories – in the end it is *people* who implement practices of prejudice and discrimination against others.

CASE STUDY

You are on placement in an inner-city early years centre. Your supervisor is Joanne, who is a qualified nursery nurse and is familiar with equal opportunities practices. Anita is a student from the local school, who is on work experience placement with you and Joanne.

During the morning break Anita tells you that she hates 'blacks'. You ask Anita why she hates black people. Anita tells you that her father hates them as well because they came over here and took all the jobs in our country, and they should go back to where they belong. (Note: The parents of the children in the early years centre were born in the UK.)

1 Is Anita prejudiced? On what information is she basing her statements?
2 Is Anita explaining her prejudice using the scapegoating theory?
3 What steps would you take to re-educate and support Anita?
4 How would you involve your supervisor, Joanne, in this?
5 Would you see Anita as a positive role model for the black children in your group? Explain the reasons for your answer.

Discrimination

Discrimination can be described as practices that have the effect of putting people of a particular group at a disadvantage. We live in a society that has a tendency to practise discrimination based on gender, race, disability, and on many other factors, such as age or sexual orientation.

Equal rights legislation (Chapter 2) highlights the fact that it is an offence to discriminate against people on the basis of their race, gender, disability or marital status. However, discrimination does still exist. Certain groups of people in society receive unequal chances and therefore find it difficult to get access to employment, good housing, adequate health care and provisions for young children.

Discrimination can be:
- direct
- indirect.

DIRECT DISCRIMINATION

This form of discrimination is practised overtly (openly). Racial and sexual harassment (see page 20) are forms of direct discrimination, as is refusing a black child or a disabled child a place on the school trip because of his or her colour or disability.

INDIRECT DISCRIMINATION

Indirect discrimination favours one group over another. It mainly takes the form of practices that are covert (hidden) – rules and regulations that make it impossible for a person belonging to a specific group to participate fully in society. For example, a supermarket chain might have a policy that states that all female checkout operators have to wear dresses. This would exclude certain groups of females, such as Muslim women whose dress code involves wearing the shalwar (trousers) and kameez (top), from competing for employment as checkout operators.

For more about direct and indirect discrimination, see Chapter 2, pages 28–30 and 35–6.

CASE STUDY

Discrimination: 1
You are on placement in nursery and you notice that the childcare worker seats all the black children together at a table. The only reason for this is that they are black.

1 Is this direct or indirect discrimination?
2 Your college tutor visits you on that day. How would you involve the tutor?
3 If you were the childcare worker, how would you change this?
4 What type of training or staff development do you think this childcare worker might need?
5 What messages is he/she communicating to the children who are not black, and to the children who are black?

CASE STUDY

Discrimination: 2

A childcare worker is holding a cookery session in the home corner. The project is 'Making a cup of tea'.

The childcare worker has asked Rashida to make a cup of tea. Rashida picks up a saucepan and pretends to fill it with water, places a tea bag in the water and asks for green cardamoms, sugar and a pinch of salt. The childcare worker explains to Rashida that she should have filled the kettle and 'no, we do not boil the teabags in the water' and 'no, we don't add bits of things to it, including salt'. However, Rashida is making tea the way it is done at home (her parents make tea in this way, adding milk later and boiling it as described).

1 What has the childcare worker done that was discriminating negatively?
2 How could this affect Rashida?
3 What aspect of equality awareness do you think the childcare worker should explore in gaining positive awareness of Rashida's lifestyle?
4 Is the childcare worker fulfilling the recommendations of the 1989 Children Act (i.e. that the child's welfare is paramount, including providing for the child's lifestyle – culture, race, etc.)?

GOOD PRACTICE

- Childcare workers must be trained in, and be fully aware of, anti-bias and anti-discriminatory practices.
- Practices should be examined and developed to provide children with equal rights at all times.

- Be prepared to challenge racism and all other forms of discrimination that disadvantage children, and be prepared to challenge individuals and their practices when necessary.
- Ask for support from the placement supervisor or the college tutor, if you feel that you need it.
- Make sure you know about the cultures and lifestyles of the children in your care.
- Do not use the practices of one culture to judge and value those of another culture.
- Remember that all cultures and lifestyles are different but equal.
- Never devalue a child's culture.
- Be a positive educator and role model.

Always value a child's culture and lifestyle.

Both the employee and the employer have responsibilities under the Race Relations Act and the Sex Discrimination Act (see Chapter 2). If unlawful discrimination is committed by an employee in the course of employment, both the employee and the employer are held responsible, regardless of whether or not the employer knew about or approved of the action. However, if it can be proved that all reasonable practicable action was taken by the employer to prevent an employee discriminating, then this may be a defence.

It is also unlawful to pressurise or to instruct a person to discriminate unlawfully. Equally, an employer who discriminates unlawfully, because she or he has been subjected to pressure, is breaking the law.

Activity
Read the two case studies about discrimination again. What are the responsibilities of the employers of the childcare workers in each case?

Harassment

Harassment is a form of direct discrimination. To harass someone means to trouble or torment them with persistent 'attacks'. Any form of harassment is illegal under civil law.

SEXUAL HARASSMENT

Sexual harassment is any harassing conduct based on the gender of the recipient. The European Commission Code of Conduct defines it as:

'Unwanted conduct of a sexual nature based on sex, affecting the dignity of women and men at work.'

Sexual harassment can take the form of unwelcome sexual advances, requests for sexual favours, or other conduct of a sexual nature, which results in the individual feeling threatened or compromised. It can be physical, verbal or non-verbal, for example gestures, leering or the display of offensive, sexually explicit material in the workplace.

For more about sexual harassment, see Chapter 2, pages 31–4.

RACIAL HARASSMENT

Racial harassment can be defined as the making of derogatory remarks, racially explicit statements that are negative, graffiti, jokes, or any action of a racist nature which is directed at an individual or group from a different ethnic background and which results in the individual(s) feeling threatened or compromised.

It might include racial comments or abuse, racist jokes or ridicule, derogatory nicknames or verbal threats. Racial harassment might also be physical.

For more about racial harassment, see Chapter 2, pages 40–3.

Are employers liable for harassment committed by their employees?
An employer is responsible for acts of harassment by employees in the course of their employment unless the employer took such steps as were reasonably practicable to prevent it. As a minimum first step, harassment of any individual should be made a disciplinary matter and staff should be made aware (in a Code of Practice) that it will be taken seriously by their employers.

'The differences between us'

All children are different, and it is this that creates their uniqueness and their individuality, which contributes to the richness of humanity.

To be different does not mean of *different worth*. We are all different, but we are all of *equal worth* – **different but equal**.

We are all different, but we are all of equal worth.

Negative attitudes and assumptions that focus on differences between us have to be addressed by childcare workers in a positive way, to prevent children's self-esteem being damaged. Equal opportunities are for everyone, and it is important that you are a positive role model, that you select resources that reflect positive images for all children in terms of books, games, play materials and equipment, posters, dressing-up clothes, cooking utensils, games, videos, TV programmes, environment, and that you use appropriate language in your communications with young children and with colleagues, because *children learn from their environment and experiences.*

If *you* use sexist, racist or disablist language, the children in your care will adopt it. You have to be careful, therefore, in your choice of language to prevent girls feeling invisible in society, boys thinking themselves automatically superior, or black, disabled or poor children feeling inferior. Language can restrict intellectual development when used to classify groups of people negatively. The challenge for you as a childcare worker is to show the children in your care that there are ways in which all children and adults will benefit by putting equal opportunities into practice.

Language is never neutral. It shapes thinking and perception, and is shaped by them. Language and inequality are closely connected, but language on its own is not responsible for inequality, nor does it hold the key for equality.

Activities
1 Look at books in use in your placement.
   a) Do you think any of them reflect negative stereotyping and discrimination?
   b) Do they portray equality?
2 Design and make a poster to use in your placement to challenge stereotypical roles and images.

The importance of equal opportunities

People who work with children should have knowledge and understanding of the principles and practices of promoting equal opportunities. Children deserve adults who are prepared to look objectively at their own attitudes and practices, to see if and how they affect children in their care, and who have the ability and courage to change the attitudes and practices that would otherwise prevent children from achieving their future potential.

We live in a multiracial, multilingual and multicultural society, and it is only natural that our children should have access to this rich heritage in their early years.

Children deserve a curriculum that is meaningful to their values, cultures, languages, race, religions, gender, disabilities and lifestyles. Young children need to explore concepts and ideas which will develop their thinking and understanding of racism, sexism, classism, disabilism and other forms of oppression.

The role of the childcare worker is important in this process. To perpetuate a sense of equality is a very serious undertaking and striving to create equality for all is not easy. However, it should not render you passive. Where inequality exists, everyone's effort is all the more necessary and urgent. *Anti-discriminatory practice means putting equal opportunities into*

The role of the childcare worker is important in promoting equal opportunities.

action. You should expect to promote these practices to give children and their families equality of opportunity. Were you to do less, you would be doing an injustice to children, their families and their communities.

Activities

1 Describe how you would promote a positive world view of children in a nursery placement setting in the following areas:
   a) the environment
   b) the curriculum.
   How could you include children's families and the community in this?
2 Explain the role of the childcare worker in the care and education of all children.

GOOD PRACTICE

- Participate in a programme of tasks to help the equal opportunities policy in your placement become a reality for all children, families and colleagues.
- Develop children's learning skills through songs and videos – experience the sounds of different languages via songs that reflect equality for all.
- Always use children and their families as sources of information.
- Create a language-rich environment for all children and encourage them to use their first language in activities.

- Present positive images of all people – ensure, for example, that black people or disabled people are shown positively in the books you use, and not as victims.
- Examine your perceptions, expectations and interactions with children, and be prepared to change your attitudes proactively.
- Have a good knowledge of equal opportunities – what it means, its policies and practices.

QUICK CHECK

1 How could children learn negative stereotyping during the socialisation process?
2 Why is negative stereotyping damaging to children's perception of themselves?
3 How could the self-fulfilling prophecy idea disadvantage a child with disability?
4 a) What are the three theoretical explanations of prejudice?
  b) Can any of the theories justify racism, sexism or disablism? If not, why?
5 How can prejudices be changed?
6 How does discrimination affect race, gender and disability?
7 Why are equal opportunities important?

KEY TERMS

You need to know what these words and phrases mean. Look back through the chapter and check that you understand:

different but equal	race
direct discrimination	racial harassment
disability	racism
disablism	scapegoating
discrimination	secondary socialisation
equality of opportunity	self-fulfilling prophecy
gender	sex
harassment	sexism
indirect discrimination	sexual harassment
negative stereotyping	socialisation
prejudice	stereotype
primary socialisation	

---

2 *EQUAL RIGHTS LEGISLATION*

> **This chapter covers:**
> - **Sexual discrimination**
> - **Racial discrimination**
> - **Disability discrimination**
> - **Equal pay provision**

Working with children and their families is an important undertaking. It is important for institutions, childcarers and students to be committed to the content of legislation and to implement equality practices, rather than just paying lip service to it. While legislation makes people aware of their legal responsibilities, it cannot, on its own, change people's attitudes, and this is particularly significant when dealing with equal rights legislation. Childcare is a public service and it is your responsibility to offer a high quality service to children and parents. This means incorporating the principles of equal rights legislation and positive attitudes into your practice. The equal rights laws discussed in this chapter require you to think beyond the 'letter of the law', and to be aware of your own attitudes and values.

High quality service reflects equal opportunities policies and practices.

Discrimination against people on the grounds of their race, gender, disability or marital status is illegal. The concept of equality was first given recognition in the 1944 Education Act. The 1989 Children Act reinforced this idea – it proposed that the welfare of the child is paramount, and that children's needs must be met, regardless of their age, sex, religion, race or ability. Children have the right to be cared for as part of a community which values their identity as individuals.

The legislation discussed in this chapter relates to the United Kingdom. However, it is not the only legislation that refers to children. There are others, such as the European Social Charter, the European Convention of Human Rights and the United Nations Convention on the Rights of the Child. These are not covered in this chapter, but you can find out about them yourself by doing some research.

The following laws are the major pieces of legislation affecting equal opportunities:

- Sex Discrimination Act 1975 and 1986 (UK)
- Race Relations Act 1976 (UK)
- Race Relations (Amendment) Act 2000
- Disability Discrimination Act 1995 and 1997
- Special Education Needs and Disability Act 2001
- Code of Practice for Special Educational Needs 2001
- Equal Pay Act 1970 (amended 1983)
- Human Rights Act 2001.

Everyone working with children should be familiar with the legislation relating to equal opportunities.

EUROPEAN CONVENTION ON HUMAN RIGHTS

The Convention on Human Rights came into force on 2 October 2001 and has had particular impact on legislation in the UK. It requires courts and tribunals to make judgments and legislation using certain articles of the European Convention on Human Rights as a starting point. While the Convention on Human Rights is not particularly aimed at protecting children, it does strengthen their rights.

Some of these laws may have a direct impact on children's lives, while others have an indirect impact. For example, the Equal Pay Act 1970 relates specifically to nursery nurses in employment.

Sexual discrimination

THE SEX DISCRIMINATION ACT

The Sex Discrimination Act (UK) 1975 and 1976 prohibits people discriminating against a person on the grounds of gender. **Sexual discrimination** is against the law in the following areas:
- employment and training
- housing
- education
- the provision of goods, facilities and services to members of the public.

The organisation responsible for administering the Act is the Equal Opportunities Commission, which has the power to monitor and investigate allegations of discrimination. The Act applies to both men and women.

You will need to be familiar with these documents in your college, placement or place of employment.

Activities

1 a) Obtain copies of the anti-sexist policies from your placement or place of work and your college.

   b) How do the policies of these organisations compare? List the similarities and differences.

   c) How effective are these organisations in putting their policies into practice?

   d) Identify teaching sessions that are good examples of anti-sexist practices in the curriculum.

   e) What recommendations could you make to improve the anti-sexist practices within the college and placement environments?

2 Make a list of job areas where men might be discriminated against. Discuss your list with other members of your group.

The Sex Discrimination Act identifies two types of sexual discrimination as unlawful:

- **direct sexual discrimination**
- **indirect sexual discrimination**.

Direct sexual discrimination

This includes explicit statements or acts, based on sex or marital status, which directly affect the treatment of people. For example, if male and female carers are employed to do the same jobs, but the women receive a lower salary than the men, this would be direct discrimination.

Indirect sexual discrimination

This consists of covert practices, which are often subtle and much less obvious than direct sexual discrimination. This happens when a

CASE STUDY

Sexual discrimination: 1

Annabel works part-time at a private nursery. She approaches her employers to talk about the possibility of training to become a nursery nurse. But the manager refuses to offer training to part-time staff. All the part-time staff at the nursery are women.

1 Under the Sex Discrimination Act, would this be sexual discrimination?

2 If it is, is it direct or indirect discrimination? Discuss this as a group.

'I am part-time, therefore I can't be trained?'

practice, such as a regulation, is not applied equally to men and women, or to married and single people. It has the effect of disadvantaging a very high proportion of the population. For example, if an employer insists that only people with ten years of uninterrupted service can be given promotion, this is indirect sexual discrimination. The women who left work to have children and then returned would not qualify for promotion.

CASE STUDY

Sexual discrimination: 2
Nadine works as a lecturer at an FE college. She has been told that she has to work from 9 a.m. to 9 p.m. However, her timetable indicates that classes end at 5 p.m. and that the students have left the premises by 5.15 p.m. The time of 9 p.m. is considered to be 'unsociable hours' and, in practice, this is never required.

 If Nadine had to stay until 9 p.m.:

1 Would this be discrimination under the Sex Discrimination Act?
2 If so, what type of discrimination is it? Indirect or direct?
3 Discuss the reasons for your answers.

CASE STUDY

Sexual discrimination: 3

Joan and Richard are nursery nurse students on placement in a day nursery. Richard is never allowed to change nappies; he is always asked to perform heavy tasks, such as lifting and moving heavy objects in the nursery.

1 Is this lawful under the Sex Discrimination Act ?
2 What type of sexual discrimination is this?
3 Should Richard be allowed to do the same tasks as Joan? If so, why?
4 What action do you suggest Richard should take when he sees his supervisor?
5 How would you support Richard positively?
6 Should Richard be allowed to continue doing the heavy tasks?

Why is Richard doing the heavy lifting, while Joan reads to the children?

CASE STUDY

Sexual discrimination: 4

A childcare worker in a nursery directs girls towards the dressing-up corner and the book corner, while the boys are directed towards the bicycles, the climbing frames, the large building bricks and the construction toys.

1 What type of discrimination is the childcare worker practising?
2 How would you address this using equal rights practices?

GOOD PRACTICE

- All workers should be treated equally, regardless of sex.
- All children should be treated equally, regardless of sex.
- Workers and children of both sexes should have equal access to experiences.
- No one should be deprived of valuable training experiences because of their sex.

SEXUAL HARASSMENT

Sexual harassment at work is unlawful under the Sex Discrimination Act 1975 and complaints about it can be made to an industrial tribunal.

Sexual harassment is any behaviour of your colleagues, which is of a sexual nature, or which is based on sex, which you find objectionable, and which has an impact on you at work. By its very nature it creates a threatening and hostile working environment.

Sexual harassment can be verbal, non-verbal or physical. Examples include:

- comments about the way you look
- lewd remarks
- questions about your sex life
- requests for sexual favours
- intimate physical contact.

What employers should do

An employer has a responsibility to ensure that sexual harassment is prevented and, if this is not possible, to respond effectively when a complaint is raised. Employers who commit or permit sexual harassment may find themselves liable for the actions of their employees under the Sex Discrimination Act 1975.

Dealing with complaints of sexual harassment at work

Receiving a complaint

Once a complaint has been made, it should not be ignored. If it is not investigated, an employer may have little defence if the complaint later proceeds to an industrial tribunal. The investigation can be carried out formally or informally but, in any event, it should be undertaken:

- immediately
- by someone who is independent and objective
- by someone with sufficient authority to take appropriate action.

Complaints of sexual harassment should not be ignored.

Informal procedure

It is obviously better for a complaint to be resolved informally, if possible. In many cases it may be sufficient to explain to the person causing offence that their behaviour is unwelcome, embarrassing and is interfering with work.

Formal procedure

If informal attempts have not been successful, or if the behaviour is too serious for the problem to be resolved informally, the matter should be pursued through a formal complaints procedure. This will require:

- the parties to be identified
- a thorough and impartial investigation of all the evidence
- each side to have an opportunity to put their side of the case, either on their own or with a friend or employed representative or some appropriate person
- consideration to be given to imposing a disciplinary penalty, if it is found that sexual harassment did occur.

Subsequent action

If a complaint is upheld, it may be necessary to separate the parties involved. However, it is important to ensure that the complainant is not adversely affected by the action taken. If the complaint is not upheld, it may still be best to separate the two parties in the interests of harmonious staff relations.

In any case, where a complaint is upheld, it is important that the employer ensures that the harassment has stopped and that there has been no victimisation – otherwise he or she may be liable in law for any subsequent acts of harassment.

Advice and counselling

Wherever possible, a person who has complained about sexual harassment should have access to someone who can give them sympathetic advice and, if necessary, counselling. This should take place in an atmosphere of total confidentiality and without pressure to take the complaint further.

Other legal consequences

Certain acts of sexual harassment may amount to unlawful assault, giving rise to civil or criminal liability. In particular, indecent assault is a serious criminal offence.

Where sexual harassment results in injury to an employee's health, or places him or her under considerable stress, the employer might be held to be in breach of health and safety duties – or of other legal duties owed to their employees – if the employer was aware of the situation (or should have been) and did not take steps to prevent it.

Industrial tribunal

A complaint under the Sex Discrimination Act must be presented to an industrial tribunal no later than one day less than three months after the alleged act occurred. If you are involved in an industrial tribunal hearing and the case goes against you, you may appeal to the Employment Appeal Tribunal. Further appeals may be made to the Court of Appeal and, finally, to the House of Lords.

GOOD PRACTICE

- Always take cases of alleged sexual harassment seriously and look into them.
- Make sure you are familiar with the procedures and responsibilities outlined in your institution's policy on harassment.
- Do not blame the victim and dismiss it as his or her fault.
- Deal promptly with the matter.
- Make sure you know what constitutes harassment.

KEY POINT

Sexual harassment is unlawful and should not be tolerated.

CASE STUDY

Janet is a female student on placement in a school, and she has complained to her supervisor, Jim, of sexual harassment by a male non-teaching assistant. The harassment consists of derogatory remarks, sexist jokes, and he has pinched Janet's bottom on several occasions. The supervisor tells her that it is her fault because of the way she dresses: 'You have been teasing him,' was Jim's reply to Janet.

Racial discrimination

THE RACE RELATIONS ACT

The Race Relations Act was first introduced in 1965 and was later amended in 1968 and 1975.

The Race Relations Act of 1965 made it unlawful to discriminate on the grounds of colour, race and national or ethnic origin in certain public places. The Act had limitations, for example it didn't apply to restaurants and hotels. The 1968 Race Relations Act extended the 1965 Act into areas such as employment, the provision of services, housing and accommodation. The 1976 Race Relations Act replaced the 1968 Act and introduced the concept of indirect discrimination to the area of 'race'.

Racial inequality is something which UK society has not successfully combated. Legislation exists to prevent people discriminating against others on the grounds of race, but these laws do not prevent people holding negative and discriminating attitudes towards 'racial' and ethnic groups.

Race Relations (Amendment) Act 2000
This protects individuals against discrimination when:
- applying for a job
- at work
- joining a club
- renting a home
- buying or selling a house
- in education and training

The Commission for Racial Equality (CRE) was set up to enforce the Act and to give advice on improving equality of opportunity in the area of race and ethnicity.

Discrimination

Section C1 of the Race Relations Act defines discrimination as:

'On racial grounds, "he" treats that other person less favourably than "he" treats or would treat other persons.' ['He' includes 'she' for the purposes of the Act.]

The Act defines 'racial grounds' as colour, race, nationality, ethnic or national origins. It does not include culture or religion. However, the 1989 Children Act does mention both the child's culture and religion.

Activity

a) Find a copy of the 1989 Children Act and read what it says about culture and religion.
b) Design and produce an activity that you could use to introduce this topic to the children in your placement.

The 1976 Race Relations Act refers to **direct racial discrimination** and **indirect racial discrimination**.

Direct racial discrimination

This means treating or telling someone that they cannot do or have something, on the grounds that they are of another 'race', colour or nationality. Direct racial discrimination is illegal.

Indirect racial discrimination

Section C1(b) of the Race Relations Act refers to indirect racial discrimination as consisting of treatment that:
- may be described as equal in a formal sense, but which is discriminatory in its effects on one particular racial group
- occurs when regulations or rules are put into practice, which are impossible for that racial group to conform to.

For example, if a nursery or school had a rule that no hats were to be worn inside the building, this would prevent certain groups of children, such as Sikhs, Muslims, Rastafarians and Jews, from accessing those places, because the rule would be impossible for those groups to conform to. The school rule would be unlawful under Section 28 of the Act, which refers to discriminating practices.

Segregation and victimisation

The Race Relations Act also defines discrimination as:

- **segregation** – setting someone (or a group) apart from another on the basis of their race
- **victimisation** – imposing sanctions on a person (or a group) on the basis of their race. For example, this might occur because a person has asserted their rights under the Race Relations Act (provided an allegation made under the Act was genuine and in good faith).

KEY POINT

It is unlawful to instruct or pressurise a person to discriminate against others, based on race.

GOOD PRACTICE

- Do not segregate children on the basis of their 'race'.
- Implement sensitive policies that reflect good practice.

Racial discrimination and employment

The Race Relations Act makes it unlawful to discriminate in employment on the grounds of race in relation to:

- arrangements made for deciding who is offered a job
- the terms on which a job is offered
- deciding who is going to be offered a job
- the benefits an employer gives to an employee, such as bonus payments and incentive schemes
- dismissals, grievances, redundancy, etc.

The exceptions to the above include when work is being carried out in private households or when race is a 'genuine occupational qualification', i.e. when race is necessary to that occupation (for example, in modelling or acting, to provide authenticity).

Within the context of employment, the Race Relations Act applies to:

- most employers and employees
- job applicants
- contract workers
- part-time and full-time employees.

Racial discrimination and advertising

When advertising, care must be taken to ensure that the wording of the advert is such that it does not discriminate against certain groups. Section 29 of the Race Relations Act deals with this area. In it, the word 'advertisement' is given a broad definition, covering the display of notices, signs, labels, etc., whether public or not. An example is given by the Commission for Racial Equality:

'It would be unlawful to publish a list of child minders known to be prepared only to mind children from a particular racial group.'

Other examples include:

- recruiting by word of mouth from friends or relatives of employees. If this excludes members of a racial group, it may lead you to break the law
- not allowing the wearing of turbans, or requiring women to wear skirts. This rules out Sikhs, or Asian women who have to wear trousers or a gown for religious or cultural reasons.

Although there is no law against religious discrimination in the UK, in some circumstances religious discrimination may be viewed as indirect racial discrimination. For example, discrimination against Muslims may be regarded as discrimination against people from Pakistan, Bangladesh or Africa, where many people are Muslims.

Positive action

The Race Relations Act does not permit reverse discrimination, i.e. it is against the law to discriminate in favour of a person or a particular ethnic group in recruitment or promotion on the grounds that members of that group have in the past suffered from adverse discrimination. However, the Act *does* permit certain forms of **positive action**, for example:

- providing access to training for a particular ethnic group when during the past 12 months, no (or very few) members of that ethnic group have been undertaking particular work
- encouraging members of an ethnic group to take advantage of opportunities for doing a particular kind of work.

However, these exceptions do not make it lawful for an employer to discriminate at the point of selection for such work.

Racial discrimination and childcare

Section 22(5)(c) of the Children Act 1989 states that local authorities have to give consideration to the religious persuasion, racial origin, cultural and linguistic (language) background of any child that comes within their care. This means that during discussions on suitable placement for a child, all the above factors must be taken into consideration.

The Children Act also makes it clear that a person's registration to care for children can be cancelled if that care provider has not responded to the needs of the child. In its definition of 'needs', the Act includes religious, racial, cultural and linguistic needs. This means that when registering a person who is deemed, under the Children Act, to be 'fit' to care for children, local authorities must take into account that person's knowledge of, and attitude to, multicultural issues, racial origins and religions.

Activity

a) Design a book about religious celebrations throughout the year that can be read to, or by, children.
b) What age group should you use it for?
c) How have you implemented various religious, cultural and linguistic needs in the book?
d) Evaluate the book based on what the 1989 Children Act says about children in local authority-governed institutions.

Special needs

It *is* lawful under the Race Relations Act for a parent to ask for a child-minder with special provisions, such as an ability to speak a particular language, if the parent is able to show a need for that provision.

Racial discrimination and education

It is against the law for an educational establishment to discriminate against a student on the grounds of race in the following areas:

- admission to the establishment
- refusal to accept an application.

Commission for Racial Equality

The 1976 Race Relations Act set up the Commission for Racial Equality (CRE). The purpose of the CRE is to act as a governing body and oversee the working of the Act in practice. It is also empowered to institute legal proceedings in respect of persistent discrimination.

RACIAL HARASSMENT

Racial harassment can be described as any action of a racist nature, which is directed at an individual or group from a different ethnic background and which results in the individual(s) feeling threatened or compromised. Racial harassment may be:

- verbal, including:
  - derogatory remarks
  - racially explicit statements
  - racist jokes
- non-verbal, including:
  - offensive gestures
  - facial expressions
  - offensive publications
  - offensive letters/memos
  - racist graffiti
  - threatening behaviour
  - threatening emails and text messages
- physical, including:

- jostling
- assault.

The offence of racial harassment is covered by Section 154 of the 1994 Criminal Justice and Public Order Act, which amended the 1986 Public Order Act. It created a new offence of:

'intentionally causing harassment, alarm or distress through using threatening behaviour or displays'.

Actions committed in public or in private fall within the scope of this offence, but behaviour by a person inside a dwelling, causing harassment to another person who is also inside a dwelling, does not.

The new offence of **intentional harassment** has been designed to deal more effectively with cases of serious racial harassment, particularly where the offending behaviour is persistent; but it applies equally to harassment on other grounds. It attracts a maximum penalty of six months' imprisonment or a fine, or both. A person reasonably suspected of committing this offence is liable to immediate arrest.

Section 155 of the Act reclassifies the offence of 'publication or distribution of written material intended or likely to stir up racial hatred' as an arrestable offence. This reclassification gives the police greater powers in investigating offences involving racially inflammatory material. They have the powers of entry, search of persons and premises, and seizure in response to:
- derogatory remarks
- racially explicit statements
- graffiti
- jokes
- any action of a racist nature which results in the individual(s) feeling threatened or compromised.

What to do if you are being harassed
- Make it clear to the harasser that you object to their behaviour:
  - in person
  - by letter
  - via a friend/colleague/manager.
- Keep a record of the incidents, dates, times, and the names of any witnesses.
- Report the harasser to someone in authority as soon as possible:
  - your manager, or someone higher
  - your personnel officer

- your trade union representative
- the Citizens' Advice Bureau.
- Then, if necessary, seek medical help/counselling.
- Follow up the complaint.
- Make a further report, if necessary.
- Seek outside help if internal disciplinary procedures are not working, for example from:
  - the Citizens' Advice Bureau
  - the Equal Opportunities Commission (EOC)
  - a law centre.
- Seek help from colleagues.
- Obtain a copy of the organisation's equal opportunities policy, if appropriate.
- Bear in mind the time limit of three months to present the case before an industrial tribunal.

Dealing with complaints of racial harassment at work
- Ensure that you are trained and up-to-date with internal procedures.
- Treat the complaint seriously and sympathetically. If necessary, ensure that another person is available to hear the complaint.
- Enquire discreetly as to whether other employees have had similar problems. If so, take details, but ensure confidentiality.
- Discuss with the complainant what action he or she wishes to take. You should ensure they know about:
  - the grievance procedure/procedure for dealing with complaints
  - their rights under current legislation and, in particular, the three-month time limit for presenting the complaint to an industrial tribunal.
- Ensure that the complainant is not victimised by colleagues or by management.
- Take prompt action to observe the time limit.
- Report the matter to the employers. They should investigate the allegation and, if appropriate, take disciplinary action. This can range from a verbal warning to dismissal.
- Keep the complainant informed as to how the complaint is being dealt with.
- Consider separating the complainant and the harasser.

CASE STUDY

Paul is a black, male, nursery nursing student on placement in a reception class in a multiracial inner-city primary school.

On Paul's first visit to the placement, he was not welcomed. The reception teacher, Mrs Jones, humiliated him in front of children and other students. He was often referred to as 'that black boy', 'come here boy' and 'that Negro boy', and seldom was he addressed by his name. He was told not to touch the white children because the teacher didn't like black students putting their hands on white children and that, if he did this, the teacher would give Paul a failed placement report, which meant that he would have to repeat the placement and have his training extended.

Paul was made to start earlier and leave later than all the other students, and his main tasks were cleaning up after the children's activities. He was not allowed to do any observations on placement, while other students were allowed the time to do so.

One day, Paul saw a child about to fall down some steps on to concrete slabs. He grabbed the child's hand to prevent him from falling. After the child was rescued, the teacher called Paul into a room in the presence of other students and shouted at him for putting his hands on a white child.

Every day the situation deteriorated until, one day, Paul walked out and went into his college to complain about the treatment he had been experiencing from the class teacher. Paul was able to produce a log recording incidents and the times and dates of his experiences. Paul even recorded the names of people who witnessed them. The childcare manager represented Paul and the matter was handled in conjunction with the head teacher, based on the college's and school's procedures for dealing with racial harassment. The teacher did not profit by her behaviour and the college supported Paul and represented his equal rights.

1 What would you have done if you were Paul? How could he have handled the situation more effectively?
2 What type(s) of harassment can you identify in the case study?
3 What types of practice did Mrs Jones participate in that were not equality practices?
4 Were Paul's feelings threatened or compromised at any time?
5 Using the guidelines for dealing with racial harassment described in this chapter, outline the procedures you would follow in dealing with the situation.

Disability discrimination

DISABILITY LEGISLATION

There are several laws in place to protect people from discrimination if they are disabled. Disability legislation:

- allows the government to set minimum standards so that disabled people can use transport easily
- set up the National Disability Council and the Northern Ireland Disability Council to advise the government of discrimination against disabled people.

Legislation affecting the care of disabled children

The Children Act 1989

This is a very important piece of legislation that affects many aspects of the ways in which children are cared for. The Act covers children who are disabled. It states that health, education and social services for children should be co-ordinated so that a seamless service may be offered.

The Disability Discrimination Act 1995 and 1997

This Act provides employment rights for disabled people and states that children with special educational needs should have school places appropriate to their individual needs.

The Act covers those who have or who have had a disability. It protects individuals against discrimination on the grounds of disability when:

- applying for a job
- at work
- buying goods and services
- buying or renting property.

No Commission was set up to enforce the Act.

Carers and Disabled Children Act 2000

This legislation came into force in April 2001. It is designed to help the people who care for children to get their needs met alongside those of their children. The idea behind this law is to help carers manage more effectively. They may be given respite vouchers as well as being offered help directly from social services.

The United Nations Convention on the rights of children states in Article 23 that a disabled child has the right to special care, education and training to enable him or her to live with the greatest degree of self-reliance and social integration as possible.

LEGISLATION AFFECTING THE EDUCATION OF DISABLED CHILDREN

The Education Act 1981

This law brought about major changes in the education of children with special needs. The main changes were:

- the introduction of the concept of 'special educational needs'
- the introduction of procedures for schools to monitor and assess children thought to have special needs, which could result in a 'Statement of Special Educational Needs'
- the requirement by law for local authorities to make special educational provision for children with special needs
- the recognition of parents as partners with the school in the education of their children.

The Education Act 1993

This is the current legislation affecting children with special educational needs. It builds on the provisions of the 1981 Act and describes the concept of 'learning difficulty' in some detail. This legislation specifically states that children should not be described as having a learning difficulty solely because their home language is not the language in which they will be taught.

Disability doesn't mean different – it means different but equal

Code of Practice for Special Educational Needs (SEN) 2001

This Code was introduced in January 2001 and supersedes the previous 1993 Code of Practice. The Code takes account of the SEN provisions of the Special Educational Needs and Disability Act 2001. The main features of the Code are:

- SEN children have more rights to be educated in mainstream schools
- LEAs (local education authorities) are required to give advice and information to parents
- settings have a duty to tell parents when they are making special educational provision for their child
- schools and nurseries have the right to request a Statutory Assessment of a child.

The Code also promotes the early identification of children who may have special educational needs. Pre-schools and nurseries are asked to draw up special needs policies and to have someone to co-ordinate special needs within the setting (SENCO).

Special Education Needs and Disability Act 2001

The Act is divided into two sections. Part One of the Act reforms the framework of SEN to strengthen the rights of parents and children to access mainstream education. Part Two expands the Disability Discrimination Act 1995 to include education, extending the civil rights of disabled children and adults in schools, colleges and universities.

The key features of the Act are:
- children with special educational needs have the right to be educated in mainstream school (where this is what parents want and where it is appropriate for the child)
- LEAs must provide parents of children with special educational needs with advice and information, and a means of resolving disputes with schools and LEAs
- LEAs must comply with the orders of the Special Educational Needs Tribunal
- education settings must inform parents that they are making special educational provision for their child and schools are allowed to request a Statutory Assessment of a pupil's special educational needs
- disability discrimination rights are now included in the provision of education in schools, further education, higher education, adult education and the youth service
- education settings must not treat disabled students less favourably, without justification, than non-disabled students.

Children with special needs are entitled to study the full national curriculum and should be given every support to do so. However, many schools and LEAs are reluctant to **statement** children under five because it can lead to 'labelling' a child at a very early age.

Integration into mainstream (inclusive education)

A major outcome of the legislation and Code of Practice described above has been the integration of children with special needs into mainstream schools. Many local authorities now have 'integration policies', which set out their plans to bring this about. Some authorities aim to get rid of all their special schools where disabled children used to be cared for all together in one place. However, many keep a small number of special schools – for example, schools for deaf children.

Integration is thought to ensure that children with special needs do not feel different, that they receive less discrimination and that other children learn to accept disability as a normal part of everyday life. However, not everyone agrees that integration is the best provision for all children.

Where children have complex and profound special needs they sometimes wish to remain in special schools where they can receive high levels of care and learning support.

Activity

a) Ask your tutor or your placement provider for a copy of the Code of Practice for Special Educational Needs 2001.
b) Make notes on any parts of the Code that you have seen being implemented in your placement.
c) Discuss this with your colleagues.

DEVELOPMENTAL FACTORS IN THE CARE AND EDUCATION OF DISABLED CHILDREN

Impairments and disabilities affect children's growth and development according to their type and severity. This chapter cannot cover the range of conditions and strategies used to assist in promoting development. Strategies to minimise the effects of disability and realise the child's potential are usually developed both for individuals and groups of children with similar needs – for example, the development of British Sign Language as an alternative first language. The social model of disability, which is now widely accepted, means that services to children with special needs must be designed to ensure that there is no barrier to the child achieving his or her full potential and this means provision of a 'disability-friendly' nursery with a range of modified and additional equipment.

Generally, play activities are graded in difficulty and the children are encouraged to move on at their own pace. All children need to succeed and should not be put into situations where they will fail. Activities with no right or wrong way of performing can build self-esteem. Small steps are best.

Professionals involved in the care and education of children with special needs

Role of the nursery nurse and other professionals
There are many professionals involved in the care and education of children with special needs. These include:
- nursery nurses
- special needs assistants
- teachers and advisers
- educational psychologists
- social workers
- speech therapists
- community workers
- health visitors
- doctors
- child psychologists
- school nurses
- physiotherapists
- play therapists.

CASE STUDY

Rehan is an insulin-dependent diabetic child attending your nursery. He comes to nursery one morning with a bag of sweets in his pocket. During the morning, Rehan becomes sluggish and falls asleep. Joanne, the nursery nurse in charge, goes over to Rehan to wake him because he is sleeping in the doorway. He does not respond.

1　What would you do?
2　Which emergency service would you call?
3　How would you involve the nursery manager?

Later in the day, Rehan's mother comes to collect him – she couldn't be found earlier. The incident is reported to her by the nursery manager. She tells the manager that Rehan didn't eat breakfast that morning because she was in a hurry, but she did give him his insulin. She didn't think there would be a problem.

4　What help and advice do you think Rehan's mother needs?
5　Do you think she fully understands Rehan's condition?
6　How could the placement provide support for Rehan and his family?
7　What other organisation do you think you could include in helping this family?

Qualified early years practitioners and nursery nurses have a vital role to play in this team. They can support the care and welfare of the whole child including health; learning and development; play; and educational activities.

Your training in observation skills is a great asset in assessing the developmental needs of children with disabilities.

Activity
Conduct a survey in your placement to identify how the placement provides for children and adults with disabilities.
a) How would a child or an adult with a wheelchair gain access to the placement?
b) What provisions are there for children with sensory impairment?
c) What kind of induction does the placement provide on its disability policy for students in training?
d) Evaluate the provisions.
e) How could the placement provisions be improved?

The Disability Discrimination Act and education

The Act builds upon the Education Act of 1993, which aims to provide all pupils with special educational needs, including disabled pupils, with an educational school place appropriate to their needs. Local educational authorities have a duty to place such children in mainstream schools, subject to the wishes of their parents, and if the placement:
- is appropriate to the child's needs
- does not conflict with the interest of other children in the school
- is an efficient use of the local education authority's resources.

Schools must continue to publish their special educational needs policies, ensuring they are readily available to parents and that a summary is included in their school's prospectus. New arrangements under the Act place a duty on the schools in England and Wales to include the following information in their annual reports:
- arrangements for admitting disabled pupils
- the ways they will ensure disabled pupils receive the same treatment as other pupils
- the facilities they will provide to enable disabled pupils to receive the same treatment as other pupils
- the facilities they will provide to enable disabled pupils to access the education they are offering.

The Disability Discrimination Act and employment

The Act makes it illegal for employers with twenty or more staff to discriminate against current or prospective employees with disabilities because of a reason relating to their disability.

Employers must not discriminate against a disabled person in:
- recruitment and retention of employees
- promotion and transfers
- training and development
- the dismissal process.

They must make reasonable changes to their premises or employment arrangements if these substantially disadvantage a disabled employee (or prospective employee), compared to a non-disabled person.

Employers can only justify less favourable treatment towards a disabled person if:
- such treatment is relevant to the circumstances of the individual case
- the reason for the treatment is a substantial one.

However, employers must consider whether adjustments could be made to overcome less favourable treatment, for example by altering the premises or employment arrangements.

Code of Practice

The Act allows the government to publish a Code of Practice that will provide practical guidance about the elimination of discrimination against disabled people in the field of employment.

Disabled people who feel that they have been discriminated against can take their case to an industrial tribunal, in the same way that has been described for racial and sexual discrimination. Industrial tribunals and courts must take account of the Code of Practice, where relevant, when considering complaints.

Activity
a) Outline the advantages of mainstream schooling for children with special needs.
b) What is 'portage'?
c) What is a 'statement of needs'?

GOOD PRACTICE

- Make sure you know about the legislation relating to disabled people and about your placement's policies, and the practices outlined in them.

- Be aware of the needs of a disabled child and ensure that you have adequate knowledge of disabilities.

Equal pay provision

THE EQUAL PAY ACT

The 1970 Equal Pay Act makes it illegal to discriminate between men and women in terms of payment and other contractual conditions such as pensions. In other words, an employee is entitled to equal pay with an employee of the opposite sex if they are doing work that:
- is the same or broadly similar
- has been rated as equivalent by a job evaluation scheme.

The Sex Discrimination Act 1975 (see page 27) also refers to equal pay – comparisons between jobs in cases of alleged discrimination cannot be made between post-holders of the same sex. They can only be made between post-holders of the opposite sex.

CASE STUDY

Anita and Nadine are employed as playgroup assistants under the same conditions of employment. One day, Nadine discovers that Anita is being paid £1.00 per hour more than she is.

1 Is this sex discrimination under the 1975 Sex Discrimination Act?
2 What would you advise Nadine to do under the 1970 Equal Pay Act?

Not all the legislation under the 1970 Equal Pay Act is relevant to child-care workers.

In 1983 the Equal Pay (Amendment) Act introduced changes in the legislation, which had become necessary as a result of proceedings made against the UK government by the European Commission. The amendments brought the UK law into line with the Equal Pay Directive and made it possible to claim equal pay for work of equal value, i.e. if the demands made on the worker were the same. For example:
- A company employs female domestic cleaners, who have the same duties as male labourers, except that the men have some additional duties such as sweeping leaves and snow. The women are paid less than the men. The women may have a claim to equal pay if the men's

additional duties are seasonal tasks, which make no practical difference to their usual run of duties.

- A female canteen cook was held by an industrial tribunal to be employed on work of equal value with that of male painters, thermal insulation engineers and joiners working for the same employer. The jobs were assessed under five headings: physical demand; environmental demands; planning and decision-making; skills and knowledge; and responsibility. The overall scores of these jobs were found to be equal.

Comparisons between jobs under the Act can only be made between post-holders of the opposite sex. Comparisons cannot be made between post-holders of the same sex.

The Act does not apply if an employer can prove there is a 'material difference' between the woman's pay and the man's, for example a London weighting allowance or a long-service payment.

CASE STUDY

Beryl and John are employed as nursery nurses in a private nursery. Beryl has the same duties as John, but Beryl is paid less than John. The jobs have been assessed and have been found to be equal.

1 What do you think would happen if Beryl were to take her case to an industrial tribunal?
2 Do you think their employer is practising discrimination? If so, what type?
3 Do you think Beryl should get the same pay as John? Give reasons for your answer.

Activities

These activities investigate employment contracts and the law. You may need to do some research of your own to complete them.

1 Under the 1989 Children Act, what is the legislation securing the protection and rights of nursery nurses in employment?
2 What are the rights regarding:
  a) the minimum periods of notice?
  b) time off work?
  c) medical suspension?

d) maternity rights?
e) unfair dismissal?
f) trade union membership?
g) guaranteed payments and redundancy payments?
h) itemised pay statements?
3 Design an employment contract for a nursery nurse. The legal requirements for an employer should be outlined in the contract.

GOOD PRACTICE

- Make sure you know how equal pay legislation applies to you.
- Be aware of gender inequalities relating to pay.
- Make sure you know about your rights and responsibilities, as set out in the relevant legislation, in relation to employment and employment contracts.

The 1970 Equal Pay Act can be found in Schedule 1 of the 1975 Sex Discrimination Act. The 'equal value' amendment can be found in the Equal Pay (Amendment) Regulations 1983, Statutory Investment 1983 no. 1794.

Guides to the Equal Pay Act are available from local jobcentres, employment offices, unemployment benefit offices or from the Equal Opportunities Commission.

QUICK CHECK

1 What does the 1989 Children Act say about:
   a) the rights of children?
   b) the culture and religion of children?
   c) the needs of children that must be met by childminders and other childcare workers?
2 An employer insists that everyone employed in an organisation has to have ten years of uninterrupted service before they could be given promotion:
   a) Is this a form of sexual discrimination?
   b) If so, what type of sexual discrimination is it? Direct or indirect? Explain your answer.
   c) Would this be harmful? If so, how?
3 What should an employer do when a case of alleged sexual harassment is reported to a line manager?
4 What are the formal and informal procedures that should be followed when dealing with complaints of sexual harassment?

5 What types of behaviour can be described as:
   a) verbal racial harassment?
   b) non-verbal racial harassment?
   c) physical racial harassment?
6 Outline how you would expect racial harassment at work to be dealt with.
7 What does the Disability Discrimination Act 2001 mean by 'disability'?
8 Summarise the main points made by the Equal Pay Act 1970 (amended 1983).

KEY TERMS

You need to know what these words and phrases mean. Look back through the chapter and check that you understand:

direct racial discrimination	positive action
direct sexual discrimination	racial discrimination
indirect racial discrimination	segregation
indirect sexual discrimination	sexual discrimination
intentional harassment	victimisation

3 PRINCIPLES OF GOOD PRACTICE

> **This chapter covers:**
> - The concept of equality
> - What is good practice?
> - Promoting equal opportunities
> - Legislation
> - Policies and codes of practice
> - Staff development
> - Good practice in the early years environment

Principles of good practice should be foremost in the minds of every adult working with young children. This philosophy should be focused on, providing children with richer life experiences and a better tolerance, acceptance and respect for each other. It should create a society that views people as unique individuals, and their differences as part of that uniqueness. Young children who experience an environment rich in good practices of equality are more privileged than those who do not. Equality encourages the individual to refuse to accept barriers that discriminate and deny them their life chances.

Education for life begins with equality, where early years experiences, based on principles of good practice, become the cornerstones for adult life. Each adult who contributes to children's experiences of equality should recognise that each child's life becomes richer for having met that adult, who offered such a selfless gift by opening the door to equality.

The concept of equality

The concept of equality is central to childcare practices. Many children and families have experienced marginalisation and oppression, and certain groups in society have been systematically mistreated and, as a consequence, access to resources in society has either been denied or limited to them. Equal rights legislation exists to prevent inequality and discrimination (see Chapter 2), but often this legislation is limited to specific forms of discrimination.

Equal rights legislation is important, but the real issue is to challenge inequality. The cure is to change attitudes, to reverse the vicious cycle of

A male nursery nurse working with children – a positive role model.

inequality, in which children are the most defenceless victims. It is the professional responsibility of all childcare workers to understand and combat inequality and discrimination. Their responsibility begins by ensuring that equality of opportunity for all exists in every aspect of childcare training, employment and education.

Society provides care for children from a variety of backgrounds – what is important is that all individuals are responded to as human beings deserving of respect and value. Negative discrimination is the cause of disharmony in our society, with much suffering for some individuals. Whatever else the progressive childcare worker does, he or she must never add to the problems faced by children and their families. The aim must be to bring down the barriers that make people prisoners of inequality – an invisible prison with invisible walls. What often eludes us is the fact that we live in a society where we are actually far more alike than we are different, and that we are all of the same worth.

One of the basic principles of the 1989 Children Act is that the welfare of the child is paramount and that all children's needs must be met, regardless of the child's age, sex, religion, race or ability. For this to be achieved, all professionals working with children must know and understand the principles relating to good practice.

What is good practice?

Good practice means promoting equal opportunities and this is achieved by implementing anti-discriminating practices. It means

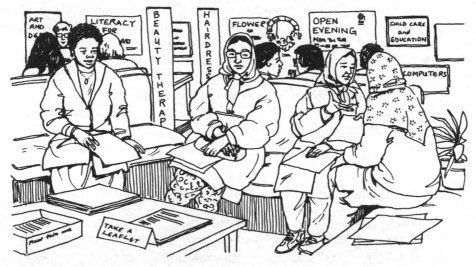

All of us should have equal chances.

putting equal opportunities into action, which requires knowledge and understanding of the principles and practices necessary to achieve the objectives. One fundamental aspect is the examination of one's own values, beliefs, attitudes and expectations. You need to analyse and evaluate these, updating and changing them when necessary, to ensure that, as a professional childcare worker or student in training, you work proactively to give all children and their families equality of opportunity at all times.

The principles of good practice involve:

● knowledge of equal rights legislation, your responsibilities under that legislation, and putting them into practice

Children learning non-stereotypical roles.

- knowledge of the organisation's equal opportunities policy and codes of practice and your responsibilities, and putting them into practice
- knowing and implementing anti-discriminatory practices
- using language and resources in the early years setting which promote equal opportunities
- on-going training in equal opportunities practices
- taking part in regular staff development, appraisal and review sessions to maintain standards of good practice.

Activity
With a partner, discuss these questions:
a) Why is the concept of equality central to childcare practices?
b) Why should childcare workers know and understand the principles and practices of equal opportunities?

Promoting equal opportunities

Equal opportunities are important because they seek to address injustices experienced by children and their families. All professionals working with children need to recognise that no one in society should be discriminated against because of their race, gender, class, culture, age, religion, disability, sexual orientation or linguistic diversity.

Equal opportunities promote positive practices to address inequalities in all aspects of the child's world. The aim is to promote equal choices, access and outcomes, along with supporting and enhancing positive **self-esteem** (respect for oneself and having the respect [esteem] of others) and **self-actualisation** (achieving one's full potential). This must be an active process – a process of doing and changing, rather than just talking about it. Communication *is* an important part of the process, but communication without action leaves discrimination untouched and unquestioned and perpetuates the *status quo*.

It is no secret that we all live in a sexist, racist, disablist society – a society that practises and perpetuates inequalities, where one section of society's life experiences are more positive than another's, with more opportunities for some and fewer for others.

Promoting equal opportunities means addressing sexism, racism, disablism and all other forms of discrimination. It involves implementing anti-sexist, anti-racist and anti-disablist practices consistently.

GUIDELINES FOR PROMOTING EQUALITY OF OPPORTUNITY

- Always remember that you are working as a member of a professional team and that all team members may have something different, yet valuable, to contribute to the early years provisions for children.
- Respect all people, irrespective of differences. See the differences as positive. Talk with people of other cultures, share common experiences and discuss differences. Consider everyone 'different, but equal'. Keep reappraising your own learning. Think about issues of race, gender and disability. Think about discrimination and anti-discrimination and how you can contribute positively to enhance changes to create richer experiences for children.
- Understand equal opportunities policies and their expectations for the individual, yourself, colleagues, your education and children's lives.
- Know how these policies affect and inform practices and be aware of your part in these processes and provisions.
- Break the habit of just talking about equal opportunities and implement a philosophy of taking action to improve practices.
- You cannot be trained to know everything – expect to ask questions and seek advice.
- Interact with children as human beings first and as having needs later. For example, don't think about the 'disabled child', the 'black child' or 'he or she', instead see the child as a human being in his or her own right – a child with a name.
- When you meet children for the first time, make sure that you have positive expectations of them.
- Value the child's family unit, whatever that unit may be. Do not be judgemental about children's families. You will meet children in family units that society has stereotyped negatively, for example, children do belong to parents who are in homosexual relationships. It is important to promote positive images of children and families from a variety of backgrounds and to acknowledge that people choose different people to have special bonding with children, so that everyone sees that their families and home backgrounds are as highly valued as all others.
- Value your own learning about equal opportunity. Know your own limitations in your knowledge and practices, and develop these proactively. Recognise that this will always be an on-going process of re-evaluation and development of your skills and practices.
- Remember that equality of opportunity is about giving every child full access to the richness of our multicultural, multiracial society.

Equality of opportunity is about giving every child access to our multicultural society.

Activities

1   Work with a partner. From the guidelines above, identify your strengths and weaknesses, and discuss how you could develop areas of weakness.

2   a) Design and make a booklet for a student on placement in a nursery giving guidelines in promoting equality of opportunity.

    b) Having made the booklet, exchange it with a colleague going into a nursery placement. Ask him or her to use it while on placement and to answer the following questions:

    ● How effective were the guidelines in the booklet when you used it on placement?

    ● How does this booklet compare with the guidelines in use at the placement?

    ● What changes should be made to the booklet, and why?

    c) As a class, discuss the outcomes of this activity.

GOOD PRACTICE

● Always know what your responsibilities are according to your placement's equal opportunities policy.

● Always implement equal opportunity practices.

● Be self-critical and make changes.

● Remember that the 1989 Children Act promotes equal opportunities as paramount to the child's welfare.

Legislation

Everyone working with young children needs to be aware of the laws relating to the care and education of all children. The most fundamental piece of legislation relating to childcare is the 1989 Children Act.

A number of laws relating to equal rights, and which have a bearing on childcare, have been introduced in the last twenty-five years:

- the Sex Discrimination Act 1975 and 1976
- the Race Relations Act 1976
- the Disability Discrimination Act 1995 and 1997
- the Special Educational Needs Disability Discrimination Act 2001
- the Special Educational Codes of Practice 2001
- the Equal Pay Act 1970 (amended 1983).

These are discussed in Chapter 2.

While we have legislation to make people aware of their legal responsibilities regarding equality, laws in themselves do not change discriminating attitudes and practices. If they did, disability discrimination, racial discrimination and sexual discrimination would not still be as widespread as they are.

Children and their families have a right to genuine commitment from professionals to the concepts and practices that underpin equal rights legislation, rather than **tokenistic behaviours**. Sometimes, people can pretend to practise equal opportunities so as not to break the law, but on closer examination their practices are found to be far from equal – equal opportunities are *seen* to be done rather than *actually* done.

The professional childcare worker is expected to offer, as part of his or her professional skills, a high quality service to children, their parents and the communities to which the children belong and where the school, nursery or playgroup is located.

Institutional and individual practices should reflect the community's needs for equality provisions in the **edu-care** of its young population. To provide such a high standard and quality of edu-care for children, all providers must be aware of their own attitudes, perceptions and values relating to equal rights legislation. The incorporation of such legislation, along with positive attitudes, must be seen as compulsory in order to reflect good practice. To fail to take this approach is to fail to provide good practice.

KEY POINTS

- Edu-care means education *and* caring.
- Tokenistic behaviour means to pretend to value something when in fact you don't. Another phrase used to describe this is 'lip service'.

Cynthia is a college tutor who is visiting a student on placement in the baby room at a local early years centre.

Janet and Firaz are nursery nursing students on placement at the nursery. The supervisor, Trisha, is holding baby Ian. Cynthia approaches Trisha to ask for some time to get a feedback on the students' progress on placement for their placement reports.

Trisha puts Ian down in the cot and, as she lays him down to sleep, Trisha says 'Don't cry, big boy!' Ian goes off to sleep. Cynthia then gets a feedback on the students; all is well.

Cynthia then asks Trisha about equal opportunity practices and how well she felt the nursery practised it. Trisha showed Cynthia posters of boys and girls playing together, photographs on the walls of black children and white children. Cynthia then asks Trisha about the remark, 'Don't cry, big boy!' made to Ian. Trisha replied, 'It's just the way I do things. Ian won't notice – he's just a baby. All he's interested in is feeding, nappy changing and a cuddle.'

Firaz was present at the time and Cynthia asked him if he noticed anything wrong. Firaz said that he couldn't see anything wrong with Trisha's statement. Cynthia then explained the concept of equal opportunities to both students and suggested that they read the early years centre's code of practice on equal opportunities, paying particular attention to anti-sexist practices.

1 Discuss your answers to these questions with colleagues, explaining the reasons for your answers if they are different:
   a) Did Trisha's language when speaking to Ian reflect discriminatory practice?
   b) If so, what type of discrimination was being practised?
   c) Why do you think Firaz was unaware of inequality practices in the baby room?
   d) Was this tokenistic behaviour by Trisha in relation to equal rights practices in the placement?
   e) What would you have done if you were Firaz?
   f) Did Cynthia deal with the situation correctly?
   g) What negative stereotyping was Trisha using?
2 If you or any of your colleagues have experienced similar situations in your placements, discuss them as a group. How was the situation dealt with?

- Never behave in a tokenistic way under the pretext of equal opportunities practices – always practice with integrity based on principles of good practice.
- Never use sexist language.
- Be prepared to challenge and discuss practices that are discriminating in your placement.
- Ask the college tutor or your supervisor for support when you need it.
- Discuss equal opportunities with your placement supervisor when being reviewed on your first meeting and subsequent meetings if necessary.

Policies and codes of practice

Every institution should have:
- an **equal opportunities policy** – a plan of action drawn up by an institution, based on its legal responsibilities and how these should be implemented
- **codes of practice** – sets of rules for the practice of particular procedures, some drawn up by individual institutions and some drawn up as part of legislation.

EQUAL OPPORTUNITIES POLICIES

An equal opportunities policy usually outlines the institution's legal responsibilities under equal rights legislation, for example, the Equal Pay Act 1970, the Rehabilitation of Offenders Act 1974, the Sex Discrimination Act 1975 and 1986, the Race Relations Act 1976, the Special Educational Needs Disability Discrimination Act 2001 and the Special Educational Codes of Practice 2001.

The policy should also outline actions and practices to be adopted by staff to eliminate direct and indirect discrimination on grounds of:
- race
- gender
- disability
- age
- sexual preferences
- culture
- learning needs
- marital status
- national origins
- criminal convictions.

In developing a policy, the institution needs to consider:
- its commitment
- the policy statement
- activities that will be undertaken, how they will be undertaken, who is covered by the policy, publicity, partnerships with the wider community, etc.
- monitoring, reviewing and action planning
- responsibilities: who is expected to undertake responsibilities in implementing the equal opportunities policy – staff, students, visitors, etc.

Guidelines on writing an equal opportunities policy
There is no specific set of rules about writing an equal opportunities policy. What follows are some guidelines to encourage principles of good practice. General policies should not be so basic that they explain too little. A good rule to follow is that you should ensure that you do not make promises you cannot deliver.

1 *Introduction* This should be a statement in the form of a short summary of the institution's policy on equal opportunities. It should summarise the organisation's position and state that the organisation recognises its responsibilities under relevant, anti-discrimination legislation, and should include a reference to whom the policy applies.
2 *Definition of discrimination* Direct and indirect discrimination should be defined, as well as victimisation and harassment (see pages 17, 20 and 36).
3 *Statement of policy* This should include sections on the following:
   - terms and conditions of employment
   - recruitment and promotion
   - training – equal opportunites training, harassment training
   - positive action – reference should be made to sections of equal rights legislation that are applicable to positive action
   - procedures for dealing with victimisation and harassment.
4 *Responsibilities for the policy* This should answer the following questions:
   - Who is ultimately responsible for implementing the policy?
   - What responsibilities do staff have for ensuring that the policy is practised?

KEY POINT

No institution can be seen as implementing principles of good practice if it disregards equal opportunities policy.

GOOD PRACTICE

- Be familiar with equal opportunities policies so that you can evaluate practices, if necessary.
- Know how to implement an equal opportunities policy (see below).
- Know how an equal opportunities policy affects children, their families and the wider community.

Implementing an equal opportunities policy

1 *Allocate responsibility*
2 *Consultation* Discuss with employees, students and community representatives the contents of the policy and its implications.
3 *Statement of policy and publicity* Ensure that the policy is known to all staff and students, including new applicants to the organisation.
4 *Training* Provide training for all staff, as appropriate, to ensure that they understand their position in law and in relation to the organisation's policy.
5 *Examination of procedures and processes* Always examine and review existing procedures and processes outlined by the policy. Modify and change where necessary to prevent all unlawful discrimination.
6 *Monitoring* Always monitor the effectiveness of the policy by regular collation and analysis of statistical data on race, gender and disability trends and population, the practices and outcomes of the organisation. Be prepared to revise if necessary.
7 *Positive action* Where the organisation is experiencing under-representation of certain groups in society, positive action should be considered and implemented following the guidelines and recommendations of the Race Relations Act and the Sex Discrimination Act.
8 *Grievance procedure* Clearly outline each stage of the procedure and the action to be taken. Identify responsibilities and deadlines in the process.

Activities

1 a) Conduct an interview with your supervisor on the placement's equal opportunities policy. Ask the following questions and add any others you can think of:
  - Where is it located within the organisation?
  - What aspect of the equal opportunity policy is the responsibility of the supervisor and how does he or she implement the policy?
  - What training has he or she had, and how often is it updated?

- What areas is he or she confident with?
- What areas does he or she think need development?
- What does the Sex Discrimination Act say about employment and equal pay?
- How does he or she reflect the Disability Act in the early years setting?

b) Analyse the findings of the interview, your observation of practices and evidence in the environment. Discuss them with colleagues in college.

2 Greenhaven is a 50-place day nursery soon to be opened in a multiracial inner-city area.

a) Design an equal opportunities policy for the nursery and outline how you would implement this policy within the nursery.

b) To whom would you allocate the responsibility for the policy?

c) What training would you provide for your staff?

d) How would you monitor the effectiveness of the policy?

e) How would you integrate the community in participating in the equal opportunity policy within your nursery?

f) Check your policy:
- Does it explain the reasons for monitoring?
- Does it include reference to the grievance procedure?
- Does it name a responsible officer?
- Does it implement equal opportunities for all (including, for example, gender, disability and race)?

CODES OF PRACTICE

Let us look at an example of a Code of Practice. The Code of Practice for Special Educational Needs (SEN) was revised and updated in January 2001 and became effective in January 2002. It replaced the 1944 Code. Local education authorities, all early years settings in receipt of government funding, health and social services departments must 'have regard' to the guidance of the SEN Code of Practice when fulfilling their statutory obligations under the Education Act (Part IV) 1966 towards children with special educational needs.

The Code recommends steps and procedures organisations must consider to enable children with special educational needs to reach their full potential, for example inputting a graduated approach of action and intervention and developing positive partnerships with parents.

This Code of Practice has at the heart of it the right of the parents and carers to be involved in all stages of planning and implementing of the child's special education needs programme. This Code also reinforces the 1944 Code in that the child is perceived as an individual, where comments are important in the process they reinforce the child's rights.

The Code of Practice guidance is informed by the following general principles:

- a child with special educational needs should have their needs met
- the special educational needs of the children will normally be met in mainstream school or settings
- the views of the child should be sought and taken into account
- parents (including those with parental responsibility) have a vital role to play in supporting their child's education
- children with special educational needs should be offered full access to a broad, balanced and relevant education, including an appropriate curriculum for the foundation stage and National Curriculum.

The SEN Code of Practice is important because it requires organisations to identify and assess children's special educational needs and to provide support to enable children to achieve their potential within the setting. Good practice involves including parents in all these processes and allowing them to contribute to the decision-making processes. The recognition of parental partnership is crucial to the relationship between the early years setting and children's families.

ISSUES: MAINSTREAM OR SPECIAL SCHOOLS?

There are many viewpoints on whether children with special needs should be integrated into mainstream school or not. Look at the viewpoints below.

- Mainstream schools can help everyone learn how to respect and value one another. Special schools make disability seem like something to be hidden away.
- Money spent on providing transport to special schools is wasted and could be used to provide better staffing and facilities for special needs children in their local area.
- Children with special needs should have the same educational opportunities as other children.
- Special schools focus attention on the disability rather than on the parts of the curriculum that children can achieve.
- Children can be protected from bullying or from being different by attending special schools.
- Mainstream schools cannot cope with children who have profound special needs. Equipment and facilities are better in special schools.
- Parents can feel more supported by each other and by staff.

Activity

In pairs, discuss how you feel about the issue of mainstream or special schools.

a) In your work placement, are there any children with special needs?

b) How does the placement respond to the needs of children with special needs?

CASE STUDY

In pairs, discuss these scenarios and create a list of the ways that you would use to promote the children's self-esteem.

1 Sika is four and lived in India until a year ago. She had polio as a baby and now uses a wheelchair.

2 Ann is three and a half and has cerebral palsy. She has some difficulty with motor skills and her speech is unclear, but she wants to join in with all the nursery activities.

3 Jack is three and has behavioural difficulties. He kicks, bites and scratches the other children in nursery and fights his carers. He refuses to use a potty and still wears nappies.

POSITIVE ACTION

Vacancies at Roseville School

We are looking for Administrative Officers to work at Roseville School.

Applicants should have 5 GCSEs, including English and Mathematics and/or have worked in an office environment for a minimum of 1 year.

The position is full-time and working hours will be either 07.30–18.30 or 10.30–21.30. We would also consider a job share arrangement.

The salary is £10,000 per annum, pro rata.

Roseville School is an Equal Opportunities Employer and we are keen to receive applications from all sections of the community. We are also a part of the Guaranteed Interview Scheme (GIS) for disabled people. If you are registered disabled and do not have the minimum entrance criteria you will be offered a guaranteed interview, which will include a test.

Please phone 01922 790345 for an application pack.

To try to balance this situation of inequality of opportunity some organisations have a policy of **positive action**. This means that they may guarantee interview candidates from a certain group. Critics of positive action say it is very unfair, while others say that this is the best way of breaking the cycle of discrimination.

Activity

1 Look at the vacancy advert showing that the organisation is taking positive action in favour of disabled people.
2 In pairs, consider what your views are on positive action.
3 As a group, discuss the following questions:
   a) What equal rights legislation would you include in an equal opportunities policy statement?
   b) Why do you need to monitor an equal opportunities policy?
   c) How would you implement an equal opportunities policy? As a childcare worker, why should you know how this is implemented?
   d) Why is training essential?
4 As a group, discuss how your placements use principles of good practice when catering for children with special educational needs?

CASE STUDY

Joseph will leave nursery soon to join a primary school. His father Peter wants Joseph to go to the local primary school near his home. Joseph suffers from epilepsy and the school tells Peter that they cannot take Joseph until he stops having fits.

1 What condition is the school practising on Joseph's admission?
2 Has Joseph got a disability?

Participation in the development of the organisation's equal opportunities policy can be made a part of the staff development programme.

Staff development

Staff knowledge and practices should be monitored and included as part of the process of staff appraisal, development and review, which should be held regularly. Staff development should work in partnership with parents and the wider community in support of the work setting.

Evaluation of practices should be regular and on-going. It is essential to ensure that staff understand the equal opportunities policy and how to implement it. It is also essential to ensure that the policy is effective and empowers staff, and that the wider organisations offer support to staff in implementation of its practices.

Staff training in anti-discriminatory practices should also be regular and on-going. All too often staff members are unsure of themselves in this area. As anti-discriminatory practices evolve, many staff remain unsure of new developments, particularly in the use of language. Words that were acceptable in the past are sometimes replaced by positive and proactive words. Staff training sessions are the best and most usual place for communicating and sharing developments in good practice.

GOOD PRACTICE

- Identify regular training days.
- Identify needs and areas of development for the organisation and its staff.
- Invite members of the community to participate with the staff team.
- Monitor and review equal opportunities practices within the work environment regularly.
- Address the needs of the team and the needs of the children, parents and community proactively.
- Invite visiting professionals to talk to staff about specific topics.

a) Develop an equal opportunities package for an induction programme for a new nursery nurse joining a nursery.
b) Identify the training you may need to provide.
c) How could you tell whether the induction was a success?
d) Why do you think new staff need this induction?

Good practice in the early years environment

Language and resources in themselves cannot promote equal opportunities – good practice is reflected in the child's *whole* environment. It is the responsibility of childcare workers to understand the principles behind the language, resources and activities they use. They should be carefully chosen and presented to develop awareness and clarify myths.

THE USE OF LANGUAGE

Language is a powerful tool whether it is written, spoken or non-verbal (gestures, etc.). It is the most effective tool of communication. If it is used positively, it can communicate respect, value, self-worth and self-esteem. It can be used to challenge. To do this, we must use the right word in the right context and remember that some meanings of words change over time – groups define and redefine words as society changes, and within groups there is a variety of words that are constantly being changed.

People need to identify who they are and not have labels imposed upon them. You will need to reflect on your attitudes, motives, feelings, thoughts and behaviour. You will need to examine your use of language and be aware of changing definitions, the reasons for these changes, and alter your use of language accordingly. Above all, when talking to others, treat them as you would like to be treated yourself – with respect.

If language is used negatively, it can devalue and belittle, it can be offensive and harmful, insulting and derogatory, it can stereotype negatively, demonstrate prejudice, be contemptuous, and lead to feelings of oppression. It can perpetuate discrimination.

GOOD PRACTICE

- Use language positively, especially in displays, stories, songs, etc.
- Value language diversity.
  - Never perpetuate the idea that the bilingual child is problematic

because she or he is competent in two or more languages. It is positive.
- Encourage children to use languages other than English.
- Let children use other languages in which they are fluent to tell stories and share in this; let them translate for you.
- Participate with parents and members of the community.
- Use a variety of languages on displays, notices and letters.
- Choose storybooks written in several languages and share these with the children. Explain what the words mean. Explain the sounds of words.
- Choose stories, books and other resources that challenge negative stereotypes.
- Language can shape children's perceptions of themselves and other children. Be aware of the words you use. For example, avoid negative uses of the word 'black', such as 'blackmail', 'black sheep of the family', etc.
- Avoid sexist usage, such as 'shy boy', 'quiet girls', 'big boys don't cry', etc. These are stereotypes. Do not use words such as 'cripple', 'wheel-chair-bound', 'spastic' – these are disablist words and phrases. Challenge language that is abusive and negative.
- Explain to children words that are appropriate and words that shouldn't be used. (Remember that children's ages and stages of development are crucial when giving explanations.)
- Consider other forms of communication that are used in society, such as sign language and Braille.

Activity
As a group:
a) Discuss and list a variety of ways of communicating with children to reflect diversity.
b) Discuss how language could reinforce negative stereotypes for children within the classroom.

CHOOSING RESOURCES

Choose resources, such as dolls, jigsaws, displays, dressing-up clothes and toys, that reflect cultural diversity. Examine packaging and enclosed literature for equal opportunity practices.

Dolls should represent racial diversity. Select carefully – it should be a genuine doll dressed in appropriate clothes, not all in celebration clothes. Black dolls should be cared for in the same way as white dolls.

Examine your behaviour – you could be conveying negative messages to the children if the black dolls are thrown in a corner of the room. Don't forget to select male dolls and dolls with disabilities, too.

Children should be aware of cultural diversity and the appropriate skills needed to reflect this. Articles such as musical instruments, cooking utensils and dressing-up clothes should not be devalued when they are used, nor taken for granted or ridiculed in jokes.

Boys and girls should have equal access to all resources.

Resources should not only reflect different races, genders, cultures and religions, they should also reflect language diversity. Disability should be reflected positively in books that you use. Positive images should be portrayed of special equipment that children may use in every-day life.

Men and women should be seen to participate in the life of the organisation: female and male doctors, male and female lorry drivers, male and female nursery nurses – all provide positive information for children.

KEY POINT

The whole curriculum should reflect equality practices.

Activities

1 As a group, discuss how the choice of resources available in the nursery or classroom could encourage children's equal opportunity awareness.
2 How does your placement reflect cultural diversity? What changes would you recommend for your placement? Compare your placement with those of your colleagues.
3 a) Design a booklet to teach bilingualism. It could take the form of a story.
   b) Read it to children in your placement and let them participate.
   c) Ask the children what they thought of the story and the new words they have used.
   d) Discuss your findings with colleagues and your placement supervisor.

It is important that all organisations involved in early years provision participate in providing positive experiences and a positive environment for all children through the principles of good practice.

● The management structure in all such organisations should reflect equal rights practices as a process of positive learning for all, providing a positive approach to race, gender and disability, reflecting the rich multicultural communities of which they are a part, creating meaningful and valuable experiences for all children.

- Behaviours and practices should reflect the organisations' equal opportunities policies and codes of practice. They should not be redundant, but *centre stage*; not in dusty, closed cupboards, but implemented in *actions*.
- Resources should be provided to facilitate the delivery of equal opportunities policy statements and children's needs should be provided for, regardless of the population the organisation serves.

Activity

As a group, discuss:

a) why equal opportunities policies should not be locked away in cupboards and unused

b) how this approach could disadvantage children and staff within an organisation.

COLLEGE–PLACEMENT PARTNERSHIPS

To perpetuate the principles of good practice, training organisations, such as colleges, should forge closer partnerships with placement providers. In the majority of cases this is happening, but this should be developed further to provide a richer training framework for students on nursery nursing programmes and develop an holistic approach to equal opportunities training for students.

QUICK CHECK

1 Why should you promote equal opportunity?

2 What is tokenistic behaviour, in relation to equal rights practices?

3 Can the individual working with young children be described as implementing equal rights practices if they are not aware of equal rights legislation? Give reasons for your answer.

4 What are the main features of an equal opportunities policy?

5 What is positive action?

6 a) Why do we need staff development in equal opportunities policies and practices?

 b) Who benefits by this process?

 c) Why include the community?

d) Why do we need to review, monitor and develop equal opportunities practices and training?
7 Why should you use language positively?
8 Why should resources used with young children reflect society's diversity?

KEY TERMS

You need to know what these words and phrases mean. Go back through the chapter and check that you understand:

code of practice	principles of good practice
edu-care	self-actualisation
equal opportunities policy	self-esteem
good practice	tokenistic behaviour

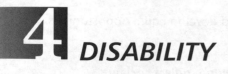

DISABILITY

This chapter covers:
- **Disability**
- **Historical perspectives on disability**
- **Models of disability**
- **Language**
- **Discrimination biases and stereotyping**
- **Professional awareness**
- **Special needs**
- **Anti-discriminatory practice**

Disability takes many forms. Some people's disabilities may be invisible and hardly affect their lives, while others' may be more obvious and more profound, to the extent that special care is needed in order to function. Disabilities may appear at birth, or may be inherited in some cases, or they may be the consequence of an illness or an accident. Whether or not they are noticeable in children, they can affect an individual's physical, mental and sensory processes.

It is not the disability that prevents disabled people from achieving a reasonable standard of living, it is the negative attitudes of other people and the policies that are made and practised that deny them their equal rights to access opportunities and life chances.

To be unable to walk is an impairment. The disability is the lack of provision and facilities, such as lifts and ramps, which can provide mobility. To deny people these basic human rights is 'society's disablement'. It is not disabled people who should be expected to change; it is society's attitudes and behaviour that should change, because this is the only way in which equality can be established.

Children are not born with negative attitudes towards disabled people – they learn them from adults, peer groups, schools, the media and the way society is organised. Unless this learning process is challenged and re-education takes place children are likely to perpetuate and reinforce the cycle of prejudice when they become adults.

- The history of disability is one of segregation, not integration.
- It is one of inequality, not equality and inclusion.

Disability

The 1995 Disability Discrimination Act defines disability as a physical or mental impairment, which has a substantial and long-term adverse effect on a person's ability to carry out normal day-to-day activities.

DEFINITIONS OF IMPAIRMENT/DISABILITY

The term impairment covers physical or mental impairment:
- Mental impairment is a term that is intended to cover a wide range of impairment relating to mental functions, and includes learning disabilities. It does not include impairments that are connected to mental illness, unless this is clinically recognised. A clinically recognised illness is one that is recognised by medical opinion, i.e. by a body such as the British Medical Association.
- A physical impairment may affect, for example, the senses, like sight and hearing, or mobility.

Disability can be described as a 'limitation in certain activities'. This goes beyond the accepted differences in ability that might exist, for example, the inability to see moving traffic clearly enough to cross a road safely, the inability to turn taps and knobs on and off, or the ability to remember and explain messages correctly.

These are limitations ('substantial adverse effects') and therefore disabilities.

Long-term effects
The long-term effects of an impairment are effects that have lasted at least twelve months or where the total period is likely to be at least twelve months or that the impairment is likely to last for the rest of the life of the person that is affected. These are effects that are likely to recur.

Short-term effects, on the other hand, are those that are likely to heal within twelve months, such as a broken leg. These are not covered by the definition in the Act.

Day-to-day activities

Day-to-day activities are defined as activities which are carried out by most people on a regular and frequent basis. The list of impairments affecting day-to-day activities is determined by whether it affects any of the following categories:

- mobility: moving from place to place
- manual dexterity: use of hands
- physical co-ordination
- the ability to lift, carry or move everyday objects
- speech, hearing or eyesight
- memory, or the ability to concentrate, learn or understand
- being able to recognise physical danger.

PROGRESSIVE CONDITIONS

Progressive conditions are covered by the definition. These are conditions that are likely to change and develop over time, for example cancer, HIV infections, muscular dystrophy and multiple sclerosis.

However, people with genes that can cause a disability are only classed as disabled if and when they develop that disability.

GOOD PRACTICE

- Be aware of the equal opportunities policies in your work placement and its practice relating to children with disabilities and **special needs**.
- Be aware of relevant procedures and what you need to know to implement these practices.
- Challenge disability discrimination.
- Ask for help when you need it.

Can you tell which of these children is disabled?

Historical perspectives on disability

Disabled people have always been part of society, but have very seldom acquired equality, often being perceived as 'abnormal', ugly or 'evil' people to be avoided. Many such people spent their lives locked away from the eyes of everyday society – rejected, often believed to be cursed, possessed by the devil or insane.

Historically, the women who gave birth to disabled children also were seen as evil, cursed or even witches. Often their children were drowned or killed. In some cultures, people with disabilities were revered as having mystical powers, while, in others, their 'affliction' was seen as God's curse for the past transgression of the parents. In feudal society, disabled people contributed positively to family life because not all were severely disabled; these children often grew up and stayed at home with parents or relatives – it was seldom expected that they would move away.

The Industrial Revolution in England created a new pattern of living and a new perception of disability, because it required families to move around the country seeking employment in industrial cities. As a consequence, people with disabilities became the responsibility of the state, and institutions, known as 'workhouses', replaced family units as places for their care.

The establishment of the National Health Service brought about changes in the life expectancies of people with disabilities. However, the 'cure' was to incarcerate people in institutions, which became their place of residence for life, and their substitute home and family in the majority of cases. Most people with disabilities who entered these institutions lived and died there.

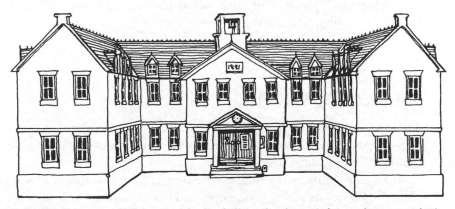

In the workhouse, children with disabilities had no rights. It became their home for life, but a home where they had no dignity.

Today, these large, long-stay institutions are less commonplace, and a philosophy of integration into the community, known as 'Care in the Community', has prompted a new approach in policy for people with disabilities. The belief, now, is that family participation in the care of people with disabilities is paramount to the individual's well-being, and more appropriate care provision reflecting people's needs is being provided.

This does not totally disregard the need for smaller residential homes in local communities, but as society is still somewhat prejudiced against people with disabilities, residents resent these provisions being placed in their own communities. Their resentment is usually based on their negative perceptions and the perpetuated myths with which they have been socialised. The consequence of such beliefs and perceptions is to deny people with disabilities their right to live life to the fullest and to be treated with respect, dignity and equality. Not all people with disabilities require such facilities, however, and provisions should be based on individual needs.

In spite of new legislation and greater awareness about disability there is still a lot to be done to achieve an inclusive and full integration.

KEY POINT

The historical perspective on disability shows inherent negative perceptions and entrenched discrimination, along with deprivation of equal rights for children and adults.

Models of disability

There are two models, which are often used as frameworks for explanations of disability. These are:
- the medical model
- the social model.

THE MEDICAL MODEL

The medical model approach proposes that disability be viewed as an illness or personal tragedy, where children and adults are seen as ill, to be dealt with by medical provision.

It sees disability as needing a cure by treatment. It does not see people with disabilities as positive decision-makers capable of being in charge of their own lives. It sees them as powerless, dependent and ineffectual. The medical model approach sees disabled people as powerless patients.

This model focuses on the disability rather than needs and emphasises treatment as a cure. Those that provide the solution are generally not people with disabilities, and if no cure is available, the solution is to incarcerate the individual in an institutional home, where others are given the responsibility for providing care for that individual.

With this model of explanation, labels like Down's syndrome and cerebral palsy are commonly used.

It socialises people with disability to take on the role of patient, dependent on others for care, powerless to take on their own responsibilities. This labelling perpetrates the role of the 'sick in need of treatment'.

These disabled children are independent and in charge of their lives. The medical model is criticised for seeing children as dependent.

Within this model society determines the care for the children with disabilities, where they should live, the schools they should access, the types of provision that should be available to them, along with their expectations of adult life and where they should expect to find employment. Children with disabilities are socialised into a culture that denies them self-actualisation; a culture that allows them no choices and no control over their own lives; a culture that ultimately reinforces a valueless self-image.

The medical model recognises the need for physical medical care, such as specialist surgery, prostheses and a range of therapies. Without medical treatment, some children with disabilities would not survive.

The medical model is seen as valuable in terms of providing relevant medical care for people with disabilities, but it is not regarded as the most popular of models for explaining disability, because it discriminates, patronises and fails to acknowledge the rights of people with disabilities. It perpetuates the labelling of people in terms of their disabilities rather than seeing them as individuals.

The philosophy of the medical model perpetuates disablism rather than equality.

THE SOCIAL MODEL

The social model of disability came about as a result of the formation of the disability movement, which campaigns for equality – a fundamental right for people with disabilities.

The social model disregards the medical approach and sees society as the cause of rejection, discrimination and prejudice. The cause of disability is seen as a lack of resources and accountability, denying people with disabilities choices and visibility, withholding their participation in the decision-making processes that affect their lives.

'I can answer the questions you're asking my father about me. I may be disabled, but I can still hear and speak.'

For people with disability to participate fully in society, society has to change in order to address these issues, and to consider the needs of people who are disabled and to make the necessary provisions for their needs to be fulfilled.

This model does not ignore the need for medical care, as this can be one component of an individual's needs. What this model advocates is that first you see people, and then you look at their disabilities. When this is acknowledged, we should see people who should participate fully in society and take charge of their lives. Society should be inclusive and the environment should be accessible, providing for everyone's rights, choices, freedom and equality.

Activities

1 As a group, discuss the following questions:
   a) How does society provide for children with disability according to the medical model?
   b) What myths about disability can you identify in this model?
   c) How does the medical model reflect equality?
   d) How does the social model see equality happening?
2 a) In groups of two or three, design a poster comparing disability as described by the social and the medical models.
   b) Using your poster, make a presentation to your colleagues on the advantages and disadvantages of both models.
   c) Identify the model you prefer, that deals with disability positively, and explain the reasons for your choice.

GOOD PRACTICE

- Do not focus on the disability – focus on the individual child and the child's needs.
- Be aware that children with and without disabilities can learn positively together.
- Speak to the person with the disability and learn from their explanations.
- Do not prejudge, and be prepared to consider new information on disability to update your knowledge.

Language

Language, whether verbal or non-verbal, is the most powerful form of communication. It conveys messages, interprets responses and facilitates interactions between individuals. It carries powerful messages, and it shapes and reflects attitudes.

When children begin to communicate, they take information from the environment and form their own perceptions. This is often facilitated by other children and family members. The socialisation process starts from birth – children who are not disabled learn to identify and label children who are usually too intellectually immature to recognise the consequences of using negative labelling to address children with disabilities, and children with disabilities are all too often fraught with anxiety and pain as a result of negative labelling and insulting words. This reinforces negative attitudes towards them and perpetuates the way society perceives disability.

Language used in books and by the media, the public, some parents, teachers, childcare workers and peer groups often contributes to the disabled child's pain, through lack of awareness of the effects of the words used.

Everyone has their own perceptions of disability, which vary according to their knowledge and experience. In your placement, you will meet children with disabilities; with some children the disability may be obvious, while with others it may take you some time to recognise that a child is dyslexic or has an illness that could affect daily activities. The language and method of communication that you and others use is paramount to the child's holistic development: incorrect and offensive words oppress, offend and patronise the child and can contribute to poor self-image and low self-esteem among children with disabilities. Always think about the words and phrases you use and choose your words with care.

The most powerful form of communication is through our interactions.

CASE STUDY

Janine is a student working on placement at an early years centre. One of the children attending the centre is Deon, who was born with one of her legs shorter than the other. She has to wear platform shoes to support her walking. One day, Janine witnessed this incident.

Deon was playing with a group of children when Stephen, one of the boys in the group, called her a 'cripple'. The children stopped playing because Deon was upset. Peter was the nursery nurse supervising the children. On hearing Stephen's remark to Deon, he looked up at Stephen but said nothing.

1 What would you have done if you were Janine?
2 How was language being used by Stephen and Deon?
3 Did Stephen see Deon as a person, or a disability?
4 How should Peter have dealt with the situation?
5 How would you explain the situation to the group of children?
6 What area of staff development would you provide for Peter, if you were the manager of the early years centre?
7 What support should the early years centre provide for Deon, Stephen, Peter and Janine to prevent further incidents like this happening?

KEY POINT

Everyday examples help children to understand differences and similarities and to learn to value these in others.

Activity

a) Look at this list of words and phrases. Divide them into those which are appropriate to use and those which are inappropriate.

abnormal	nutter	cripple
deaf and dumb	mongol	the deaf boy
stupid	mental	that baby with cerebral
lunatic	spastic	palsy

b) Compare your answer with a colleague's. Do you agree? Discuss any differences.
c) If any of these words were used to address you, how do you think it would make you feel? Discuss this with colleagues.
d) Which words in the list focus on the child, and which focus on the disability?
e) Create a list of positive words to replace those above.

GOOD PRACTICE

● Never assume that a child with a disability cannot understand you.
● Always treat children as individuals and respond with due respect.

- Never allow other children to tease or use negative name-calling to their peers.
- Respond appropriately to inappropriate behaviour from others.
- Always ask the individual how they wish to be addressed/referred to and be guided by his or her response.
- Words like 'handicapped' are denigrating – use the child's name.
- Think positively – do not project the image of 'victim' on to the individual.
- Do not refer to people who use wheelchairs as 'wheelchair-bound'.

ANTI-DISABLIST LANGUAGE

Introduce the topic of disability in discussions with groups of children; if a child has a disability, let him or her lead and educate others. Children are naturally curious and are aware of disabilities – some very young children may see a child with a disability as different. Children need accurate and appropriate information, taking into consideration their ages and stages of development. If questions are not answered honestly, this may reinforce children's anxieties and fears, and also reinforce myths about disabilities that they already hold, which in turn could perpetuate negative attitudes, biases and discrimination. Children often imitate language used by adults and other children. You should, therefore, be aware of the appropriate language used in addressing disabilities.

KEY POINTS

- Always use appropriate language yourself and teach children the correct words.
- Positive words communicate value and respect to children.
- Words can be powerful tools of discrimination.

'Come on Andy – join us!'

Activities

1   Obtain a copy of your placement's disability policy. It will outline practices.

a) What evidence can you see in your placement that reflects a positive approach to disability? Is the policy being fully implemented?

b) Examine the reading materials available in the placement. Do they reflect equal opportunities policy on disability?

c) Identify examples of good practice in your placement.

d) Discuss the positive and negative findings you have discovered in your placement with colleagues at college.

e) What changes in practice would you recommend?

2   As a group, discuss the following questions:

a) Why is it important to respond to children who use disablist words?

b) Why should you be honest in your explanation to children when they ask you about disability?

c) How could you disadvantage a child with disability by using inappropriate words?

GOOD PRACTICE

- Use positive language.
- Treat children equally.
- Be prepared to change your attitudes.
- Be prepared to work effectively with parents and families.
- Do not criticise children because they are curious and ask you questions about disability.
- Know the new legislation on disability.

Discrimination biases and stereotyping

Discrimination may be practised by an individual or by a group of people. It results in different and unequal treatment, and is often a result of negative stereotyping. The effects of discrimination on a child with disability and special needs can be profound – dejection, feelings of powerlessness, loss of self-esteem, loss of motivation and loss of self-confidence.

Discrimination begins with the negative biased attitudes of others and creates victims, who begin to behave in the ways expected of them. This reinforces initial prejudices and a vicious circle is created. This vicious circle is only broken by changing attitudes. Turning vicious circles into virtuous circles should be an essential task of all childcare workers.

Discrimination and prejudice on the grounds of disability or special needs must be challenged. Children who are being discriminated against by name-calling, or by being alienated from an activity, should be supported, comforted and issues should be discussed with the child, to allow the child to talk about how they feel in an open and honest way. The children practising this form of discrimination should be reminded that it is inappropriate practice through role play, and through stories and small group activities the early years worker should explain and reinforce what is acceptable behaviour and what is hurtful to other children.

Labels and stereotypes that focus on disabilities highlight the differences between groups of people, attaching a superior/inferior label to children – 'them and us'. For example, children with disabilities may be seen as weak, helpless victims looking for sympathy, unable to express choices or opinions, in need of care from others who are more capable.

CASE STUDY

Daniel is three years old and attends nursery. He wears a calliper and has to walk slowly, sometimes losing his balance and falling over. He has no problems communicating in two languages – English and French.

One morning, Daniel's uncle brought him to nursery. Erma, the nursery nurse, greeted all the children and then went over to Daniel and his uncle. Daniel said 'Hello' to Erma, but she ignored him and began to talk to his uncle. One of the questions Erma asked the uncle was 'What does Daniel like to eat?' Daniel's uncle wasn't sure and tried to ask Daniel, but Erma continued, 'What is Daniel's favourite food?' Daniel answered, but Erma wasn't listening to his replies. Daniel, feeling ignored, walked off into the nursery to take off his coat and put it on his peg and started to cry. Erma went over to Daniel and rebuked him for walking off while she was talking to his uncle. Daniel continued to cry.

1 Was Erma implementing practices that reflected equality for Daniel?
2 Identify the element of Erma's behaviour that discriminated against Daniel.
3 Why do you think Erma asked the uncle about Daniel's likes and dislikes about food, instead of asking Daniel himself?
4 What was Erma's attitude portraying?
5 What action could you take in supporting Daniel?

6 If you were Erma's supervisor and you witnessed this incident, what action would you take in addressing this with Erma?
7 How would you involve Daniel's uncle?
8 Having addressed the questions above, discuss your answers with colleagues and feed back positive actions that you would implement in your placement in addressing children with disabilities following the new legislation.

GOOD PRACTICE

- Always challenge discrimination proactively.
- Avoid the use of negative stereotyping and address this when it occurs in children's and adults' language.
- Encourage all children in the nursery to be involved and share in activities.
- Use anti-bias and anti-discriminating practices.
- Know the new legislation on disability.

PROFESSIONAL AWARENESS

The child with disability is entitled to equality at all times. As a professional, you should always be aware of policies and practices that reflect this.

Talking to the carer (as in the case of Daniel and his uncle) instead of talking to the child is unacceptable and can have a negative effect on the child and the family. Assuming that a child is deaf or unable to understand and communicate, and being preoccupied with the child's disability rather than his or her ability, are all unacceptable behaviour.

Lack of awareness of disability is extremely negative for any child or adult. Disability awareness should focus on the needs of the child and their families and carers.

GOOD PRACTICE

- Both parents and childcare professionals should listen and talk to children with disabilities and learn from what they say.
- Recognise the need for an environment that reflects equality – one that is inclusive, accessible and positive.
- Displays, play materials, literature and music must reflect positive images of children with disabilities.
- Ensure you have adequate and relevant knowledge to challenge all forms of discrimination, such as language, name-calling, inappropriate behaviour, negative stereotyping, direct and indirect discrimination.

- Staff development and listening are essential for equal opportunities practice.
- If necessary, ask for help.

KEY POINT

Higher staffing levels are important in an inclusive setting to care for children requiring help in fulfilling their needs, e.g. mobility, eating, drinking, etc.

Special needs

Under the 1989 Children's Act, children with special needs are categorised as 'children in need'. The idea of a special needs categorisation has caused a good deal of confusion between parents and professionals. Experts have indicated that it should be assumed that special needs, by definition, allows children's needs to be met.

The most useful aspect of the special needs categorisation is to facilitate provisions for children with special needs, particularly those provisions that are seen as the responsibility of local authorities and schools. Children with special needs are now being included into the mainstream more than ever before, due to the new legislation Special Educational Needs and Disability Act 2001 (SENDA) and SEN Code of Practice. It is likely that, during your training, you will participate in some aspects of their everyday life, whether your placement is in a nursery, reception class, a school, a playgroup or in the home environment. You will be part of a team of professionals that responds to and satisfies children's everyday needs. You may even want to specialise in special needs care as your area of interest. Many nursery nurses select this path during their training.

The term 'special needs' is used in the childcare setting to describe children that are different but equal. We know that, generally, children tend to follow a pattern of development concurrent with ages and stages. However, it is now recognised that not all children follow this pattern and not all children reflect similar ages and stages of development. Children with special needs are at different points in their developmental stages.

There are many types of special educational need. Many children can have short-term special needs, caused by such things as parental separation and divorce, moving to a new home or new area, the loss of a sibling or the arrival of a new baby – children do experience emotional trauma. These needs require expert skills to support the child positively; if these needs are not dealt with adequately, it can in some cases have debilitating consequences, such as behavioural problems, emotional, social or learning difficulties.

DEFINITION OF SPECIAL EDUCATIONAL NEEDS

Children have special educational needs if they have a learning difficulty, which calls for special educational provision to be made for them.

Children have a learning difficulty if they:
- have a significantly greater difficulty in learning than the majority of children of the same age; or
- have a disability, which prevents or hinders them from making use of educational facilities of a kind generally provided for children of the same age in schools within the area of the local education authority
- are under compulsory school age and fall within the definitions above or would fall into this category if educational provision was not made for them.

Children must not be regarded as having a learning difficulty because the language or form of language of their home is different from the language in which they will be taught.

Special educational provision means:
- for children of two or above, educational provision is additional to, or otherwise different from, the educational provision made generally for children of their age in schools maintained by the LEA, other than special schools, in the area
- for children under two, educational provision of any kind.

QUICK CHECK

1 Which Education Act sets out the current legislation for children with special needs in England and Wales?
2 What do you understand by the term 'special educational needs'?

THE SPECIAL EDUCATIONAL NEEDS AND DISABILITY ACT 2001 AND REVISED REGULATIONS

The Special Educational Needs and Disability Act 2001, and revised regulations, came into effect on 1 January 2002. It places new statutory duties on LEAs, schools and early years settings, with regard to special educational needs, additional to those set out in the Educational Act 1996 (Part IV), for example:

- a stronger right for children with SEN to be educated in mainstream school. Reinforcement of the right of children with physical and behavioural difficulties to be taught in mainstream classes
- the requirement for LEAs to provide advice and information services for parents of children with SEN, and offer a means of resolving disputes
- schools and relevant nursery education providers must tell parents when they are making special educational provisions for their child
- the right of schools and relevant nursery education providers to request a statutory assessment of a child.

Part II of the Special Educational Needs and Disability Act 2001 places additional anti-discrimination duties on LEAs and schools. From September 2002 schools cannot treat disabled pupils less favourably because of their disability, and must take reasonable steps to ensure that they are not placed at a substantial disadvantage compared to those who are not disabled.

KEY POINT

A Disability Rights Code of Practice for Schools, prepared by the Disability Rights Commission, gives new practical guidance for implementing these new anti-discrimination duties. This Code should be used alongside the Special Educational Needs Code of Practice.

THE SPECIAL EDUCATIONAL NEEDS CODE OF PRACTICE 2001

The Special Educational Needs Code of Practice became effective from 1 January 2002. It replaces the 1994 Code. Local education authorities, all early years education settings that receive government funding (including private nurseries, pre-schools and accredited childminders working as part of an approved network), and health and social services departments, must 'have regard' to the guidance in the SEN Code of Practice when fulfilling their statutory duties; it does not tell settings what they must do, but it does recommend the steps and procedures they must consider to enable children with special educational needs to reach their full potential – for example, implementing graduated approach of action and intervention and developing positive partnership with parents. The Code of Practice builds on the rights of parents to be involved in all stages of planning and implementing their child's special educational needs programme.

The guidance in the Code is informed by the following general principles:

- a child with special educational needs should have their needs met
- the views of the child should be sought and taken into account
- parents (this includes all those with parental responsibility) have a vital role to play in supporting their child's education
- children with special educational needs should be offered full access to a broad, balanced and relevant education, including an appropriate curriculum for the foundation stage and National Curriculum.

(Quoted from the Special Needs Code of Practice 2002).

'Having regard' to the SEN Code of Practice will be a new experience for many early years providers and practitioners. Information, advice and support in interpreting and implementing the Code is provided by Local Education Authority Development Officers, Early Years and Childcare Partnerships and the Parent Partnership Service provide.

KEY POINT

The manager or head teacher of an early years setting, working closely with the SEN co-ordinator, is responsible for the overall provision for children with special educational needs. The delegation of particular responsibilities is a matter for individual settings.

FACTS ON IMPLEMENTING THE SEN CODE OF PRACTICE

Special Educational Needs Policy

All maintained schools, and early years providers delivering government funded early education, are expected to develop and publish a Special Educational Needs Policy, whether or not they currently care for a child with SEN. The SEN Policy must take account of the SEN Code of Practice. Private and non-maintained early years education settings may wish to draw up and publish an SEN Policy. Accredited childminders, who are part of an approved network, may work together to develop an SEN Policy.

Advice for providers who are undertaking writing a policy can be obtained from LEA Development Officers, Early Years and Childcare Partnerships, Parent Partnership Services and other neighbourhood early years settings. Special Educational Needs Policies will be structured to meet the needs of individual settings, but should contain a Policy Statement (the aims of the setting); Organisation (roles and responsibilities of the staff within the setting); and Arrangements (how you carry out your aims). The format and wording of the policy must be user friendly and easy for staff and parents to understand. All practitioners in the setting work together to develop an SEN Policy, there is a sense of shared ownership and greater commitment to a successful implementation of the policy. Settings may wish to consider suggestions from parents for inclusion in the policy. When necessary, the policy must be available in different languages, large print, Braille or on tape.

A summary of the SEN Code of Practice, guidance for early years settings follows.

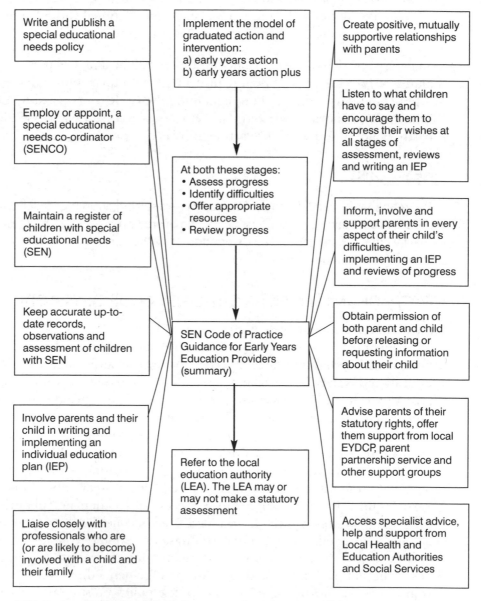

SEN Code of Practice for early years education providers.

FRAMEWORK FOR A SPECIAL EDUCATIONAL NEEDS POLICY

Policy statement

In the Policy Statement a setting will include a commitment to:

- the ethos of inclusion, difference and diversity
- writing the aim and objectives of the setting with regard to children with SEN
- early identification of children with SEN
- encourage and assist children with SEN to reach their full potential
- establish positive partnerships with parents
- provide the organisation and arrangements for implementing the SEN Policy
- provide resources for SEN support
- provide staff training relating to SEN implementing the SEN Policy
- provide resources for SEN support
- provide staff training relating to SEN issues.

Organisation

An organisational chart naming the members of the early years team and stating their titles is helpful for staff, parents and external specialists.

The responsibilities and duties of each member of the team should be described in detail.

Arrangement

The setting should describe (among other things) the arrangements for:

- developing an inclusive approach within the setting
- welcoming children with SEN and their parents to the setting
- providing interpreters, translators, signers and ethnic link workers when necessary
- physical access – modifications and adaptations
- identifying and assessing children's special educational needs
- delivering the curriculum
- Reviewing children's progress
- accessing and allocating resources, co-ordinating provision
- creating links with external agencies, for example, health and social services, Early Years Development and Childcare Partnerships (EYDCPs), Parent Partnership Service, voluntary organisations and other special needs support groups
- creating a partnership with parents and informing them of their rights
- maintaining confidentiality both within the setting and with external specialists and agencies
- staff training
- resolution of disputes.

SPECIAL EDUCATIONAL NEEDS CO-ORDINATOR (SENCO)

All early years education providers must employ an SEN Co-ordinator, or designate an existing member of staff to take on the role and responsibilities of SENCO. For accredited childminders the role of SENCO may be shared between the co-ordinator of their network and individual childminders.

The SENCO works closely with the head teacher, or manager, and other colleagues and is responsible for monitoring and co-ordinating the SEN Code of Practice. Below is a summary of the roles and responsibilities. The SENCO should:

- oversee the day-to-day operation of the SEN Policy, maintain the SEN register and accurate, relevant, up-to-date records of individual children
- co-ordinate provisions and support for children with SEN at stages Early Years Action and Early Years Action Plus, also at stages School Action and School Action Plus
- make sure appropriate Individual Education Plans (IEPs) are in place and implemented
- collate and present relevant records, assessments, observations and progress reports to the LEA when a child is referred for Statutory Statement
- liaise with parents of children with SEN and with specialists from outside agencies who are involved with the child and her family, for example, the LEA psychology service, health and social services and voluntary organisations
- provide parents with information about services offered by the LEA, the local EYDCP and Parent Partnership Services, and other local voluntary and support groups
- support and advise the early years team, contribute to in-service training of staff and, with the manager or head teacher, arrange staff training on issues such as Code of Practice, writing a Special Educational Needs Policy, disability, equality and other relevant subjects.

GOOD PRACTICE

The confidentiality code of the organisation must be maintained when dealing with information; parents' and carers' wishes must be respected at all times.

PARTNERSHIP WITH PARENTS, CARERS AND CHILDREN

Those in parental roles have a good deal of knowledge about their children and have a critical part to play in their education. A positive, trusting and supportive partnership between the setting, the parents and the local education authority is central to a child's education and overall progress. The SEN Code of Practice puts greater emphasis now on the involvement of parents in all decision-making processes, such as identification of their child's SEN, action and intervention programmes, review processes and assessments. It is important that the early years team takes time to listen to parents' views and concerns, and welcomes the knowledge and expertise they can offer about their child. All professionals and specialists attending the child in the setting or in the community (physiotherapist, occupational therapist, speech and language therapist, educational psychologist, support teachers), as well as early years practitioners, rely on parents to reinforce and consolidate care and learning plans in the home. The process of statutory assessment and making a statement of special educational needs can be an anxious time for parents. They may require support at all times and need to be kept fully informed on the range of available local provision, including schools. At the time of a proposed statement of special educational needs, local educational authorities *must* remind parents about the Parent Partnership Service and the dispute resolution services.

I am not excluded, I am part of the team!

THE NEEDS OF THE CHILD MUST BE PARAMOUNT

The SEN Code of Practice states that children have important and relevant information to offer about their education. Always encourage children, including very young ones, to express any wish or difficulty and prompt them to make even the smallest choices and decisions. Avoid making assumptions about the level of understanding of any child. Older children may welcome the opportunity to talk privately about their education. Children of any age, with learning, communication or sensory difficulties, may need extra help to make their views and wishes known. For children who are unable to express a wish or choice, or have no one to speak on their behalf, the services of an advocate should be provided.

GRADUATED RESPONSE ACTION AND INTERVENTION

Where a child is experiencing particular or general learning difficulties, the early years setting or school should offer that child different opportunities or alternative approaches to learning.

The early years graduated approach
Children's progress is monitored and assessed throughout the early years foundation stage of education (from the age of three years to the end of the reception years). If a child appears to be experiencing general or particular learning difficulties the early years setting will need to consider different approaches and procedures to assist learning and help the child to make progress.

The Code of Practice recommends two stages of graduated action and intervention in the early years settings:
1 Early Years Action
2 Early Years Action Plus.

Early Years Action
Good practice can take many forms and early years providers are encouraged to adopt a flexible and graduated response to the special educational needs of individual children. Some children's special educational needs will be met simply by adapting approaches and targeting the learning more carefully; others may require higher levels of support and differentiation and the early years organisation might bring on board specialist expertise if the child is experiencing continuing difficulties.

Once a child's special educational needs have been identified the providers should intervene through Early Years Action. Early Years Action is the first stage of intervention aimed at helping a child who is experiencing learning difficulties. When the early years team or SENCO identifies a child with special educational needs, they provide interventions that are *additional to* or *different from* those provided in the setting's usual curriculum.

Triggers for intervention through Early Years Action

The early years team, or a health or social services professional, might be concerned that a child, despite receiving appropriate early learning experiences:

- makes little or no progress, even when teaching approaches are structured to meet the child's identified needs
- works at levels far below those expected for children of similar age, in certain areas
- exhibits persistent emotional and/or behaviour difficulties, which are not relieved by the behaviour management strategies in place in the setting
- has poor communication and intervention skills, which require specific learning support
- has sensory or physical problems even when provided with personal aids and equipment.

Having identified the triggers for intervention the early years practitioner should speak with the parents and carers; a shared programme from the beginning and a welcome and positive atmosphere for the families will make the process easier for all.

The early years practitioners should discuss their concerns with parents or carers and offer support or help via the SENCO. Parents or carers should be encouraged to discuss any issues or concerns they might have about the child (e.g. behaviour, health, physical development, etc.) and any difficulties they might be experiencing.

The SENCO then liaises with external specialists who could already be involved with the child's case. Accurate records of the child's progress and specific needs will be required, including observations of behavioural difficulties and specific gathering of evidence to support reasons for concerns.

THE INDIVIDUAL EDUCATION PLAN

Once thorough evidence has been gathered, the SENCO and early years team will discuss with parents and carers and the child an Individual Education Plan (IEP). This individualised approach is devised to help the child achieve maximum learning and progress (see the example of IEP proforma on page 108). An example of what a completed IEP might look like for Hyacinth, a child with significant emotional difficulties, can be found on page 102.

An IEP should set out any particular teaching strategies that are additional to or different from the differentiated curriculum plan that the child already follows. The IEP also identifies particular short-term targets for the child, specifies a review date and records the outcomes when the IEP is reviewed. Arrangements and resources for teaching and learning strategies may include individual, group or out-of-hours support (breakfast or lunch-time clubs); different learning materials or special equipment; LEA support services for advice on strategies or equipment; and LEA staff training to provide effective intervention without the need for regular and on-going input from external agencies.

KEY POINTS

- Partnership with parents and carers and children is paramount in the process.
- The key to Early Years Action is effective individualised arrangements for teaching and learning.
- An IEP must be changed and restructured without waiting for the next review date if little or no progress is made. Always discuss with the parent the child's progress and why the IEP is being changed.
- An IEP is reviewed frequently – at least once every term, or more frequently if necessary.

Activity

In small groups, look at the IEP on pages 102–3:
a) What barriers do you think the parents could have in participating in the IEP process?
b) Is the IEP addressing Hyacinth's needs?
c) How would you improve this IEP?
d) Discuss and feed back to your class.

Early Years Action Plus

What happens if the early years team has been taking Early Years Action for a child who has SEN and the team feels that the child is not making the progress that he or she might?

This kind of decision would normally arise out of one of the regular review meetings.

Early Years Action Plus triggers

The SENCO and early years team seek help from external support services when, despite following an individualised programme and/or concentrated support, the child:

- continues to make little or no general progress in certain areas over a long time

- follows an early years curriculum well below that expected of children of similar age
- has physical or sensory needs and requires additional special equipment and/or support from external specialists
- displays emotional or behavioural difficulties that substantially and regularly interfere with the child's own learning or that of the group, despite an individualised programme for behaviour management
- experiences on-going communication and interaction difficulties that adversely affect social relationships and learning
- has sensory or physical needs and requires additional equipment or regular help from an outside specialist.

The SENCO, early years team and parents meet to review the child's IEP and discuss on-going difficulties and needs. A request for help is made to the external support services and all relevant information (observations, assessment or test results, IEP and progress reports) is made available to them. It is likely a specialist will observe the child in the setting and then offer advice on a new IEP, identify particular targets and teaching strategies; provide more specialist assessments; advise on the use of new or specialist materials; and provide support for particular activities. Parents are consulted and involved in drawing up the IEP.

External support services for early years settings in the maintained sector can be accessed through the LEA Special Educational Needs Officer, the local health authority or social services department. Specialists include: the paediatrician; the educational psychologist; support teachers for sensory, learning or behavioural difficulties; speech and language therapists; and physiotherapists. Technicians are also available to support children with physical and/or sensory impairment.

KEY POINTS

- The different kinds of advice and support available to early years settings may vary nationally.
- The two-stage early years graduated approach of action and intervention is based within the early years setting.

QUICK CHECK

1 What is the SEN Code of Practice?
2 Identify two principles in the SEN Code of Practice relating specifically to parents of children with special educational needs.
3 For what reason would early years staff implement (a) Early Years Action and (b) Early Years Action Plus?

Regular reviews

The IEP needs to be reviewed regularly. There is a proforma on page 108, which can be used or adapted. Parents and carers should also be asked to contribute using the proforma on page 103.

Name: Hyacinth	Early Years Action/Early Years Action Plus

Nature of difficulty: Hyacinth finds it hard to settle in the group, even though she has been with us three terms. She is extremely quiet and shy and lacks confidence to join in with other children. Hyacinth does not speak at nursery.

Strength: Hyacinth likes to be with Sadia, one of our regular staff.

Action: Sadia will continue to be Hyacinth's keyworker. She will greet Hyacinth each morning and take her to sit quietly in the book corner while the other children settle. Sadia will play alongside Hyacinth in the quiet room with a small group of other children, helping her to play and interact more socially and giving her confidence during new play activities. If Hyacinth is tearful, she can sit quietly with her teddy bear in the book corner, with Sadia close by but not always cuddling her.

Who by? Sadia

Help from parents or carers: We assured Hyacinth's parents that she could bring her favourite toy to nursery as a comforter. Hyacinth's parents will come in to spend a whole session with her in nursery, so that she can show off all she is doing there. Hyacinth's parents will look for opportunities to invite other children from the nursery in to play at the weekends. Sadia has offered to visit Hyacinth at home in the early evening in order to play with her in a more boisterous mood and also to make an observation of her language. Hyacinth's parents will bring her in five minutes early when the nursery is still quiet. Sadia and parents will keep a two-way diary so that they can keep more closely in touch.

Targets for this term:

Personal, social and emotional development: Hyacinth will come into nursery without crying	Knowledge and understanding of the world: Hyacinth will show curiosity during topic work and watch a group of other children investigating.
Communication, language and literacy: Hyacinth will talk freely with Sadia when playing one-to-one in the book corner	Physical development: Hyacinth will join in a movement game in a small group, holding Sadia's hand.
Mathematical development: Hyacinth will join in the action of a simple number rhyme when sitting next to Sadia.	Creative development: Hyacinth will paint independently for five minutes, even if other children approach.

Any pastoral or medical requirements:
We are not certain whether Hyacinth's speech and language skills are developing, as they should be. Perhaps she finds it hard to understand words and routines that are not familiar to her. We will discuss our assessments with her health visitor.

Monitoring and assessment arrangement:
As soon as Hyacinth has achieved these targets, we will extend them so that she begins to interact
and speak with other children. We will record her language, looking particularly at how well she can understand Sadia's instructions and share this with the health visitor.

Review meeting with parents or carers: In half a term
Other people to invite: Health visitor

Sample of a completed IEP.

Name of your child: _____

At home
When does your child need most help at home?

About the group
Is your child happy to come to the group?

Are you worried about anything to do with the group?

How do you feel about your child's progress?

Do you feel your child's needs are being met?

Health
How has your child's health been lately?

Are there any changes in medication or treatment?

The future
What would you like to see your child learning to do next?

Are you worried about anything in the future?

What questions would you like to ask at the review?

What changes would you like to see following the review?

Parent's contribution to review meeting template.

KEY POINTS

- The key to Early Years Action is effective individualised arrangement for teaching and learning.
- An IEP must be changed and restructured without waiting for the next review date if little or no progress is made. Always discuss with the parents the child's progress and why the IEP is being changed.
- An IEP is reviewed frequently – at least once every term, or more frequently if necessary.

A child with identified SEN is unlikely to have received a statement of special educational needs in an early years setting; however, the school should have access to earlier records and IEPs, which will have been written in the context of the Foundation Stage curriculum.

A 'pupil record' for a child with SEN in infant school includes information about a child's progress and behaviour from the school, the child's early years education setting, parents and health and social services.

The SEN Code of Practice sets out a two-stage process of graduated action and intervention for children in infant school. The stages are School Action and School Action Plus.

SCHOOL ACTION

The first stage of intervention is School Action, which is aimed at helping a child who is experiencing learning difficulties. Interventions that are *additional to* or *different from* the school's usual differentiated curriculum are implemented by the class teacher and the SENCO.

Triggers for intervention through School Action

School Action is indicated when the class teacher or SENCO identifies that a child:

- makes little or no progress and experiences difficulty in developing mathematics and literacy skills, even with a specially targeted teaching approach

- displays persistent emotional or behavioural problems, which are not relieved through the behaviour management strategies of the school
- experiences sensory or physical difficulties although specialist equipment is provided; or has communication and/or interaction difficulties even with a differentiated curriculum.

Interventions include writing an IEP that sets out particular teaching strategies and provisions, short-term targets, review date and the outcomes when the IEP is reviewed. To help the child to progress, group or individual support may be offered and different learning materials and equipment provided. The class teacher remains responsible for working with the child on a daily basis, and for planning and delivering an individual programme.

SCHOOL ACTION PLUS

The second stage of intervention is School Action Plus, which is aimed at helping a child who is experiencing learning difficulties. Following a review of the IEP by the SENCO, teachers and parents, a request for help from external support services (curriculum, literacy and numeracy co-ordinators and external specialists) is made.

Triggers for School Action Plus
School Action Plus is indicated if a child continues to:
- make little or no progress and works at National Curriculum levels well below that expected of children of similar age
- experience difficulty with literacy and mathematics skills.

WHAT HAPPENS NEXT?

Statutory assessment
A statutory assessment is a detailed multi-agency review and consideration of a child's special needs and necessary educational provision. Early years settings and schools, in consultation with parents and external specialists, may request the LEA to make a statutory assessment if, despite intervention and help through Early Years Action and Early Years Action Plus or School Action and School Action Plus, a child has not achieved progress and there is significant cause for concern.

The SENCO and external specialists fully discuss the details of assessment with the parents and child. LEAs decide whether or not to make a statutory assessment only when they have: studied reports and assessment and evidence of achievement in the early learning goals; reviewed documentation and IEPs from all those who have been involved with the child; assessed all the identified difficulties the child is experiencing; and examined the intervention strategies implemented by the early years or school settings.

If a decision to make an assessment is made, a named LEA officer acts as a source of information between the LEA and parents. Parents are also entitled to independent advice and help throughout the process of assessment. A Named Person and Independent Parental Supporter (IPS) can offer support to parents by attending meetings with them, encouraging them to participate with the professionals' discussions on their child's behalf and helping them to understand the SEN framework. The Named Person or IPS may be someone from a voluntary organisation, the local Parent Partnership Service, another parent who perhaps has a child with special needs and understands the system, or a friend.

Following statutory assessment, the LEA decides whether the child's needs can be adequately met by the early years setting's or the school's resources or to make a statement of the child's special educational needs.

If the LEA decides *not* to make a statement, a 'note in lieu' is usually sent to the parents explaining the decision and recommending further appropriate provision for their child.

STATEMENT OF SPECIAL EDUCATIONAL NEEDS

A Statement of Special Educational Needs is a legal document detailing a child's special educational needs and setting out the provision the LEA considers necessary for the child. It forms the basis for the child's future education plans. The framework of a statement is included below. Parents are advised that Parts 2, 3 and 4 of a statement are legally binding on the LEA, but Parts 5 and 6 are not. A draft, or proposed, statement is sent to the parents. If they accept it, the contents become final and a copy of the completed statement is given to them. The time taken from the statutory assessment to the final statement must not exceed twenty-six weeks.

As far as possible, arrangements are made for a child's education to continue in a mainstream school of the parents' choice. For some children with multiple and complex SEN, the facilities, specialist teaching, expertise and adapted environment of a special school may be of greater benefit.

Name of child:
Date of review meeting:
Who was present?
Who has spent reports (attached)?
Progress since the last review:
Any special support arranged:
How helpful has this been?
Any recent changes in the situation?
Have the targets on the previous IEP been achieved?
Negotiate and attach the current IEP:
Date of next review meeting:
This review report has been circulated to:

Progress review template: Early Years Action/Early Years Action Plus

Name:	Early Years Action/Early Years Action Plus
Nature of difficulty:	
Strength:	
Action:	
Who by?	
Help from parents or carers:	

Targets for this term:

Personal, social and emotional development:	Knowledge and understanding of the world:
Communication, language and literacy:	Physical development:
Mathematical development:	Creative development:

Any pastoral or medical requirements:

Monitoring and assessment arrangement:

Review meeting with parents or carers:

Other people to invite:

Individual education plan template

Reviewing the statement

A Statement is reviewed every year (every six months if the child is under five years). It may last for the whole or part of a child's school career. It ceases at sixteen if the child leaves school at that age. An LEA may maintain the statement if a child remains at school until nineteen years of age.

Provision of resources identified in a statement can be expensive. Budgets are generally over-stretched and tightly controlled. It is often felt that a statement is resource-led rather than needs-led and parents may express concern that their child is not receiving the level of support indicated in the statement.

KEY POINT

It is the duty of LEAs to decide *whether or not* statutory assessments should be made. It is also their duty to *make* both statutory *assessments* and Statements of Special Educational Needs.

Writing the statement

A Statement has six parts.

Part 1 *Introduction*: The child's name and address and date of birth. The child's home language and religion. The names and address(es) of the child's parents.

Part 2 *Special Educational Needs* (learning difficulties): Clear details of the nature and severity of each and every one of the child's special educational needs, as identified by the LEA during statutory assessment, and of the advice received and attached as appendices to the statement.

Part 3 *Special Educational Provision*: The special educational provision that the LEA considers necessary to meet the child's special educational needs.
   a) The *objectives* that the special educational provision should aim to meet.
   b) The *special educational provision*, which the LEA considers appropriate to meet the needs set out in Part 2 and to meet the objectives.
   c) The *arrangements* to be made for monitoring progress in meeting those objectives, particularly for setting short-term targets for the child's progress and for reviewing the child's progress on a regular basis.

Part 4 *Placement*: The type and name of school where the special educational provision set out in Part 3 is to be made of the LEA's arrangements for provision to be made otherwise than in school.

Part 5 *Non-educational Needs*: All relevant non-educational needs of the child as agreed between the health services, social services or other agencies and the LEA.

Part 6 *Non-educational Provision*: Details of relevant non-educational provision required to meet the non-educational needs of the child as agreed between the health services and/or social services and the LEA, including the agreed arrangements for its provision.

Signature and date.

(Taken from the Special Educational Needs Code of Practice)

Advice attached to the Statement *must* include educational, medical, psychological and social services advice, plus advice the LEA has asked for from any other body and considers to be relevant. Parental evidence and any views expressed by the child are also included.

KEY POINTS

- The recommended special educational provision identified in Part 3 of a Statement may include speech and language therapy, learning support assistance or specialist equipment.
- Non-educational needs in Part 5 of a Statement may include physiotherapy or occupational therapy or help to develop self-care and independence skills, mobility training or respite care.
- The actual provision set out in Part 6 may include arrangements for particular therapies and respite care, and a special needs assistant to help with self-care and independence skills.
- In exceptional cases, special travel arrangements may also be provided.

QUICK CHECK

1 Who is resonsible for writing a Statement of Special Educational Needs and making a statutory assessment?
2 What must the advice attached to a Statement always include?
3 Against which parts of a Statement of Special Educational Needs may parents (a) appeal and (b) not appeal?
4 How can a special school be more appropriate for some children with special educational needs?
5 Describe the non-educational needs a child could have.

STATUTORY ASSESSMENT AND STATEMENT FOR EARLY YEARS CHILDREN

Children under compulsory school age and over two years

Health authorities and National Health Service (NHS) Trusts must inform parents and the appropriate LEA if they consider a child under compulsory school age and over two years may have special educational needs (Section 332, Education Act 1996). A child development centre may provide a multi-specialist assessment of the child's difficulties. The LEA will want to know about the difficulties identified by the early years setting (if the child attends one) and whether or not outside specialist help for the child's physical health and overall development has been requested. If a child's educational needs appear complex and likely to be on-going, or there is a need for specialist intervention to support the child's difficulties and developmental delays, then it is likely the LEA will make both a Statutory Assessment and a Statement of Special Educational Needs. The Statement will follow the same format as for older children (see above).

Children under two years

When a child under two years is referred to the LEA it is likely that a parent or the child health services have first identified a special need. **Sure Start** may also identify a child with special needs and co-ordinate access to appropriate services. A Statutory Assessment for a child under two years can only be made if a parent gives consent for it. An LEA must make the assessment if a parent requests it. An assessment at this age is generally based on medical and developmental observations made in a child development centre.

A Statement for a child under two years is rare. However it may be appropriate if a child's needs are complex or if it will help the child to access a particular service or area of support that is needed.

Special educational provision for children under compulsory school age includes:

- the Portage Home Visiting Programme
- peripatetic teacher support for children with vision or hearing impairment
- advice from a clinical or education psychologist for a child with behavioural difficulties
- attendance (or continued attendance) in a mainstream early years setting
- attendance in a specialist setting

The LEA and local EYDCP hold information on nursery school/class provision for children with SEN, also the availability of places in a range of early years settings such as family centres, day nurseries and playgroups in the area.

For children and families for whom English is not their preferred language, LEAs should provide information through translators, interpreters and signers, on tapes and in Braille (according to need), at all stages of intervention and action (both in early years settings and schools), and during the procedures of a Statutory Assessment and a Statement of Special Educational Needs.

KEY POINTS

- Any concerns the staff in an early years setting may have about a child's developmental progress should be shared as early as possible with the parents or carers and the local education authority.
- Parents must be kept informed, involved and consulted at all times throughout the decision-making processes concerning their child.

Activity
A child with a Statement of Special Educational Needs is shortly to attend the school where you work. What does this mean for the child? What particular responsibilities do the class teacher and early years worker have to undertake?

SPECIAL EDUCATIONAL NEEDS TRIBUNAL

The Special Educational Needs Tribunal considers appeals by parents against local authority decisions about their child's SEN. It is an independent tribunal, unconnected to any local education authority. A decision is made after considering all written and verbal evidence, including whether the local education authority has acted within the guidance set out in the Code of Practice. The government cannot influence the tribunal's decisions.

Reasons for an appeal

- If the local education authority decides against making a Statutory Assessment or does not make a Statement of Special Educational Needs after a Statutory Assessment.
- Against the description of a child's special educational needs and/or the special educational provision the local education authority has identified.
- Against the school named in the statement or the refusal of the local education authority to change the school named in the statement.
- If the local education authority refuses a request for a further assessment or ceases to maintain a statement.

KEY POINT

The following conditions cannot be the basis for an appeal: the way the local education authority carried out the assessment; the length of time the assessment took; Parts 5 and 6 of a Statement of Special Educational Needs; or the way the early years setting or the school is meeting a child's special educational needs.

Activity

What do you think would influence parents in the choice of school for their child who is the subject of a Statement of Special Educational Needs?

CASE STUDY

Anisa is seven years old and her parents, John and Niketa, have identified that she isn't reading as well as other seven year olds in her class. They believe that Anisa's reading age is that of a four year old. They have expressed their concerns to the school, but the school does not respond. Anisa is becoming depressed because she is unable to keep up with the reading and with the other children.

Using the Special Educational Needs Code of Practice:
1 What advice would you give John and Niketa?
2 How would you propose to help Anisa, if you were a classroom assistant attached to the class that Anisa is in and you were asked to work with Anisa one morning?
3 Are Anisa's needs being met by the school?

A partnership with parents is essential for quality care of children with special needs and disabilities.

Anti-discriminatory practice

This should always be a positive approach. Working with children *and* their families is very important for the child with a special need. Most children are loved by the family to which they belong, whatever constitutes a family for the child. However, this is not the experience of every child, where family members may not be fully aware of aspects of the child's disability or special needs. For a child experiencing limited mobility, the family and carers are the ones that they depend on for help and support.

People working with children with specific needs must be aware that children have the right to be individual, the right to be cared for, to be loved, valued, respected and the right to feel secure.

Children's all-round developmental needs must be addressed. The play environment, equipment and facilities available should be suited to the child's needs. Specialist care, both professional and medical, as well as integrated education and day-care provision, should reflect all needs of children positively.

A child's special needs should not be perceived as the child's main focus point because this in no way enhances his or her development or meets his or her needs. This approach only serves as a platform for voyeurism, further reinforcing the notion of the 'child in need', of a sense of sympathy and helplessness.

Partnership between parents and carers is essential for the child's holistic development. Some parents may need help to understand that they should provide children with independence rather than over-protection and self-blame.

Clio is a child with sickle-cell anaemia. She suffers at times while at the nursery, and the nursery nurses and managers are fully aware of her needs.

In the nursery, Clio is expected to explore, interact and participate with all aspects of the nursery life; she is not restricted and, here, Clio shows independence. Clio's father, John, usually collects her in the afternoons. He always arrives half an hour early, stays in the nursery and plays with Clio and the other children.

One afternoon, Kathy, the nursery manager, watches John, Clio and a group of children playing. Clio wants to roll out some dough, but John refuses to let her do it – he rolls it out for her. He stops Clio from walking about when she wants to and lifts her up and takes her around the nursery. Clio protests and wants to be put down on the floor to walk. John doesn't let her and she starts to cry. Kathy goes over to John and suggests that he join her for a cup of tea, whereby John places Clio on the floor and she goes off with her friends. In the conversation with Kathy, John tells her that he is frightened in case Clio gets hurt.

1 What is John doing that could be seen to be preventing Clio from being independent?

2 How would you explain the balance that is needed between John's caring and protecting approach and Clio's need to develop her independence?

3 Was Kathy's action necessary? And how did it help John and Clio in dealing with the situation?

4 How would you help John to provide a more appropriate response and approach to Clio's needs?

5 Design a booklet for the nursery and for parents explaining a positive approach for children with sickle-cell anaemia. Test its effectiveness on your next placement and feed back to your colleagues and supervisor at college.

Parents and carers need help and support, but they are not the only ones – other members of the child's family may need help and support too. This can be shared with professionals caring for and educating children. The child and the family could be a source of support and information. Whatever the approach, always see it as the 'whole child approach' – not just in terms of the disability or need. Children need to be encouraged to approach disability and other needs positively; poor self-image should never be attached to a child. If a child has low self-esteem, help him or her to form a positive view of him/herself.

POSITIVE ACTIONS

Use these positive actions to combat discrimination and promote equality for disabled children and their families:
- Always use the child's name – do not label the child by his or her need or disability.
- Use an **inclusive approach** in the placement, i.e. include all children in activities, do not exclude any.
- Use positive language.
- Do not have or encourage low expectations of children.
- Challenge negative stereotyping, inappropriate language and discrimination.
- Encourage the child to reach her or his full potential.
- Encourage independence, decisions and choices.
- Be aware of all children's needs.
- Create and provide appropriate physical environments inside and outdoors.

During the last few years, more and more playgroups, nurseries and pre-school provisions have been rethinking their practices and policies relating to disability and special needs. The new approach is one of inclusiveness and integration. This shows recognition of the value of children's equality and is a positive approach. However, it may not be the provision needed by some children and families.

> **Activity**
> a) Write a code of practice for your placement on the inclusive approach for all children (including disability and special needs).
> b) How would you prepare staff to implement it?
> c) How would children participate and gain positively as a result of the code of practice?
> d) How would you monitor the effectiveness of your code of practice in providing equality for all children?

RESOURCES

Resources, such as toys and play equipment, the curriculum, pictures, displays, posters, books, music, stories, songs and TV programmes should all be carefully selected to reflect equality. Allow children to explore all resources, and explain their use clearly and honestly.

GOOD PRACTICE

- All staff should have relevant up-to-date training in equality practices and care for children.
- Special skills are sometimes needed, such as the ability to use sign language or to speak other languages, because, far from the negative perception, the bilingual or multilingual child is not a disadvantaged child – it is a highly complex intellectual achievement to transfer learning skills and words from one culture to another in order to communicate effectively. Transferring language from culture to culture with appropriate meaning is very sophisticated – particularly when one of the cultures has no appropriate words for what is being perceived, only an approximation.
- Do not exclude any child.
- Offer play equipment that reflects an holistic approach for all children.
- Meet the needs of all children equally.
- Allow children and families to get involved in sharing experiences about needs and disabilities – break down barriers of myth and fear by talking and responding positively to questions that children may ask.
- Above all, *you* need to be a positive role model, as children copy adults' behaviour.

Do not exclude any child – meet the needs of all children equally.

QUICK CHECK

1 How do the following view disability:
a) the medical model?
b) the social model?
2 Why is language important when communicating with children?
3 Why is it important that you use appropriate words when referring to children with disabilities?
4 What are the categories of special needs?
5 Identify some causes of special need, both long-term and short-term.
6 What are learning difficulties?
7 What is the Special Educational Code of Practice, and what does it do?
8 What are the stages of assessment?
9 What positive actions can you take to promote equality for children with disabilities and special needs?

KEY TERMS

You need to know what these words and phrases mean. Go back through the chapter and check that you understand:

disability   special educational needs
impairment   special needs
inclusive approach   statementing
individual education plan   statutory assessment

GENDER

Children's attitudes are seen as a reflection of what they see adults doing. Even as early as primary school, most children are aware of the roles of men and women in society. As recently as 1992, a survey showed that, out of some 500 five year olds interviewed, 95 per cent of the boys believed that repairing cars should be done only by men, while 86 per cent of the girls in the research indicated that they thought that only women should sew clothes.

Historically, male and female roles were seen as quite distinct. However, things are slowly changing as some fathers are beginning to take more interest in the care of their young children and more women are going out to work. Attitudes about women in employment are changing. Consequently, the role of day care for children becomes important and valuable, benefiting both the children and parents in terms of children's social, intellectual and educational development, with positive early years experiences outside the home. It is the quality and stability of the care that the child receives that is of importance, and not necessarily mothers' care and attention that contributes in this preparation for a world in which women and men play more equal roles, both in the home and at work. Childcare workers should be forging partnerships with parents in effectively providing this experience. Eliminating negative gender stereotyping in the child's early years will be of lasting benefit to girls and boys, influencing an educational and social development that is more positive in maintaining their self-esteem.

What is gender?

One of the most common questions asked at the birth of a baby is, 'Is it a girl or a boy?' Evidence suggests that parents still have preferences and, to some extent, it is still believed that the first-born should be a boy, in order to carry on the family name. In some sections of society today, the birth of a girl is not as important as the birth of a boy.

The new-born baby's **sex** can have far-reaching consequences for the older child's, and later the adult's, life experiences. It is a kind of prediction that she or he will follow one of two very different developmental pathways – one that might not always reflect equality for that child.

Children are born into a society that already has an established culture, with norms, values, beliefs, attitudes and behavioural expectations of its individuals based on their **gender**. It is from this society that children's ideas are formed, a society where inequality is still being perpetuated and where the superiority of one gender and the inferiority of the other is often commonplace.

Gender and sex are often used as if they have the same meaning, but they do not. These terms need to be clearly defined in order to focus our thinking, otherwise concepts, issues and perceptions become blurred and confusing.

KEY POINTS

- Sex is a biological definition and refers to genitalia. It is usually seen as unchanging (but can be changed by surgery). For example, a sex difference is that men cannot bear children.
- Gender is a label that is socially-constructed and can vary in different cultures. It is the product of socialisation, and refers to the psychological and cultural aspects of maleness and femaleness. For example, a gender difference is that men do not (usually) take responsibility for childcare.

Sex and gender differences can become confused when discrepancies occur in our beliefs and expectations. For example, biologically, women have an external layer of fat under their skin to protect them from the cold, while men do not (a sex difference). But men are expected to behave 'as gentlemen' by lending women their coats or jackets to protect them from the cold (a gender difference).

The term 'gender-typing' means categorising according to perceived male and female characteristics.

Activities
1   As a group, discuss whether a persons's sex always reflects their gender.
2   a) List four examples each of gender-typed:
- toys
- professions

- roles in the house
- personality characteristics
- social behaviour.

b) Discuss with a colleague your reasons for classifying as you have. Were you ever unsure about your classification?

GOOD PRACTICE

- Be aware of the difference between sex and gender. Remember that biological sex does not always reflect appropriate gender.
- Be aware of society's influence on gender inequality and practise gender *equality* at all times.
- Ask for help if and when you need it.

In the UK, gender inequalities continue in spite of equal rights legislation such as the Sex Discrimination Act 1975 and 1986, and the Equal Pay Act 1970 (see Chapter 2). Under this legislation, it is illegal to practise sex discrimination in education, housing, training, employment or other such areas.

Girls and boys are not treated equally, which disadvantages them and stops them fulfilling their potential. The challenge to all professional childcare workers is to enrich children's experiences by presenting girls and boys with opportunities to gain positive perceptions and expectations of themselves and of each other.

One aspect of 'self' is the child's sex identity. The knowledge they acquire about their sex is learned from early infancy. This learning process is reinforced in their everyday life. Young children are not cognitively (mentally) mature enough to realise that their sex has certain biological implications for their future behaviour, and that their sex is unlikely to change as they grow up.

In society, there are certain forms of behaviour that are still regarded as appropriate for one gender and inappropriate for the other. For example, it is seen as 'normal' for females to be gentle and emotional, but not males, who are supposed to be tough and physical. This **gender role** behaviour can place either gender in an inferior or superior position and, generally, it is seen that girls and women experience less superior positions within many cultures compared to boys and men. Men *do* experience inequalities, for example in childcare training and employment in the early years sector.

However good our intentions are to value children and respond to their individual needs, intentions alone are not sufficient. We need to

'We like being mechanics.'

look at the child's environment to see what messages are being communicated to them by the way your placement is staffed and managed, because staffing reflects role models for children and affects their future expectations.

> **Activity**
> Conduct a survey of staffing in your placement:
> a) What sex are the carers, helpers and nursery nurses?
> b) What sex are the cleaners?
> c) What sex are the caretakers?
> d) What sex are the cooks?
> e) What sex are the maintenance people?
> f) What messages are these communicating to young children?
> g) Compare and discuss the results of your survey with colleagues' surveys.
> How similar are your findings in relation to gender and roles? For example, are the cleaners in all the placements surveyed female?

Sex stereotyping

Sex stereotyping is a term often used when discussing equality of opportunity in child development. We have already seen, in Chapter 1, that stereotyping is the over-generalised way of labelling people long before we really know them – it is an assumption we make about them, based on incomplete information and misinformation. Sex stereotyping is such an assumption based on a person's sex. For example, we might assume that all women will have babies, simply because they are female and only females can have babies.

Stereotyping is a way of communicating information in a compact form. We can use a stereotype as a label to describe something that will be easily understood by others in society. The stereotype can include a great deal of information.

However, stereotyping is inherently negative, because it limits and defines experiences before they happen. When we use stereotypes, we fail to see exceptions and we ignore alternatives to the stereotype. To go back to the example of women having babies, this stereotype ignores the fact that some women cannot have babies, some choose not to and some, due to their circumstances, just don't have them. This stereotype has been used by some employers, who deny female employees the opportunity of further training or promotion because they assume that they will eventually leave to have children. This assumption limits women's career chances.

THE EFFECTS OF SEX STEREOTYPING

Sex stereotyping has negative and damaging consequences because the underlying assumption is that an individual's sex is a form of limitation and definition of their future experiences. Childcare workers' and parents' attitudes to boys and girls may be significantly influenced by stereotypes that they hold about gender roles. For example, they might encourage boys' learning, but feel that a girl's education is not so important – because a girl's role is to get married and have a family!

In reality, the differences between individuals of one sex (boys, say) – in terms of strength, interests, scientific or mathematical ability, for example – may be just as great, possibly even greater, than the differences between girls and boys.

Assumptions based on stereotyping can result in carers, parents and teachers misperceiving the abilities and potentials of the individual child. The consequence of this is that boys and girls do not achieve their aspirations because adults' expectations limit children's learning, and it is children who suffer the consequences, to their lasting detriment.

Sex stereotypes are commonplace in society. By the age of three or four, many children are aware of sex stereotypes. Research indicates that children of this age group can identify different clothing that men and women wear – i.e. men wear trousers and shirts, while women wear dresses and carry handbags – and also that men do different jobs to women – i.e. men dig trenches, repair cars, etc., while women clean the house and iron the clothes.

In 1978, a researcher called Kuhn and colleagues conducted some research with children aged two and three on stereotyping males and

What aspect of this picture reflects traditional gender roles?

females. They found that as early as two years old, children had knowledge of some stereotypes. The children believed that girls liked dolls and preferred domestic duties.

Other research suggests that, in western cultures, these stereotypes and beliefs about the sexes are consistent across children of all ages and social backgrounds. It is reflected in the media, books and television programmes for children and adults.

Cross-cultural studies also support the patterns of sex stereotyping in young children. Research in 30 different countries, including adults and children, indicated that most children aged five and eight had identified men as aggressive, cruel and adventurous, and women were seen as affectionate, gentle, emotional, weak and dependent. Hence the widespread shock that occurs when a woman is found to be involved in a case of child abuse – she is not conforming to the widely-held stereotype of female behaviour.

Research has shown that girls are influenced to adopt passive roles from an early age, while boys are encouraged to be aggressive and competitive.

Researchers in the 1980s looked at the influence that gender stereotyping has on children's play. They found that pre-school children often have strong ideas about what girls and boys can do and that some play activities are dominated by one sex more than the other. Not all the children participate in all of the activities, because some are seen by children as being suitable either for girls or for boys. This could influence girls and boys in having limited views of choices available to males and females in society.

Girls are boisterous and capable as well – look at the girls in this playground.

USING LANGUAGE TO COMBAT SEX STEREOTYPES

Good practice is based on examining attitudes and languages used when dealing with boys and girls from an early age. Language can reinforce gender stereotypes, as in expressions such as 'boys don't cry', 'girls should not play rough and tumble', or 'Aren't you a tomboy!'

By reinforcing sex stereotypes we only succeed in limiting children from learning new and innovating experiences. Pre-school children are learning all the time from the rich environment around them. They learn to understand the vast amount of information they receive by classifying that information into groups. So, they learn about groups such as men/women, girls/boys, and about attitudes and behaviour ascribed to these groups. The choice of words you use with young children can, therefore, be very influential. If you refer to teachers as 'she' and doctors as 'he', you are suggesting to the child that teachers fit into the female group while doctors fit into the male group. It does not tell the child that males and females can fit into either group, because no further information is provided for the child.

Language used in classifying can restrict children's lives, so girls should not be socialised to feel invisible in society or boys into thinking themselves automatically superior.

You should help children open doors in terms of power, personality and future occupation by including 'she' when you would usually and automatically say 'he'. Explaining the language you use when speaking to young children is paramount.

Activity

a) Observe two children's television programmes suitable for children aged four years, and record how they portray male and female roles. If you have a video recorder, you could record the programmes and analyse them, taking notes to address the following questions:
- What roles do the females play?
- What roles do the males play?
- Are there any examples of traditional gender roles, either in the activities or in the use of language or the behaviour portrayed?
- How are they socialising young children with reference to what males and females should do?

b) Critically evaluate the programmes:
- What is negative about them (i.e. inappropriate or sexist examples)?
- What is positive about them (i.e. good examples)?
- How could they be improved in portraying a positive image to girls and boys?

KEY POINT

Boys and girls should be treated as equal.

- Do not use negative gender stereotyping.
- Activities should not be selected based on whether they are suitable for boys or girls.
- Provide new experiences for children to extend their knowledge.
- Always implement anti-sexist practices.

Learning through play helps to develop equality for children – we build together, we learn together.

Theories of gender role development

Debate still continues about how a child learns gender identity and roles. Three of the main theoretical approaches, which aim to explain the origins of gender role development, are:

- psychoanalytical theory
- social learning theory
- cognitive development theory.

PSYCHOANALYTICAL THEORY

This approach sees biological differences as the key to gender development. The best known of these is Sigmund Freud's psychosexual theory. Here, genital differences determine the psychological characteristics of males and females. According to Freud, males and females start out neutral and later learn to identify with the same sex parent after becoming aware of their own biological characteristics.

Erikson's research with young children and construction-building tasks indicated that girls tended to construct structures reflecting inner space, such as rooms, whereas boys reflected outer space, such as towers. Erikson's conclusion from this research was that it reflected children's anatomical features.

Explanations of behavioural patterns based on anatomical features are highly questionable. Using physiology and anatomy as determinants for behaviour begs the question of reliability and validity.

The psychoanalytical approach is deeply rooted in the individual's biology. But what these theorists have failed to address is how the child came to learn the social significance of biological differences. As a theory of gender acquisition, it is highly unreliable and open to much criticism and controversy. It can be said to be *scientifically unreliable*.

Activity

Why would psychoanalytical theory be unreliable in explaining gender role development? Discuss your answer with colleagues.

SOCIAL LEARNING THEORY

Social learning theory is based on the idea that children learn gender behaviour from the society they live in and from the expectations of people around them. Children learn these behaviours through the process of reinforcement and modelling, and in so doing children's behaviour is shaped towards that of males and females. This is done by rewarding boys and girls for appropriate behaviour and discouraging inappropriate behaviour.

Research in the 1950s by Sears and colleagues found that mothers allowed boys to express aggression far more than girls. Boys were encouraged to be assertive, to fight back, while girls were severely punished if they attempted the same thing.

Later studies in the 1970s found similar patterns. In one study, babies were dressed in pink or blue, according to whether they were male or female. Mothers were filmed interacting with the babies. The babies in blue tended to receive more stimulation from the mothers than the babies in pink. Mothers would offer the babies in blue assertive type toys, such as hammers, and the babies were jigged and bounced up and down, while the babies in pink were patted and soothed and expected to lie quietly and play with soft cuddly toys. This research showed that parents may be establishing different behaviour patterns for boys and girls quite early in life.

Fathers and mothers do react differently to children's gender behaviours. In research in 1978, parents were seen to treat boys and girls differently. Fathers were seen as more likely to play rough and tumble games with boys, than with girls. Parents were seen to show more approval when children behaved appropriately to their gender, and responding negatively when children behaved inappropriately.

Social learning theory proposes that children's behaviour is shaped by the behaviour of others – especially parents – and that one's gender differences in behaviour and attitudes are learned by observation, imitation and reinforcement. Parents and others reward appropriate behaviour and discourage, or disapprove of, inappropriate behaviour. In addition, children observe other people's behaviour – especially people of the same gender – and it is this that they imitate. This is called **observational learning** or **modelling.**

CASE STUDY

Brenda is a nanny employed to take care of Jack, aged two-and-a-half years, and Anabel, aged three-and-a-half years, while the parents work full-time.

One day, when Brenda is preparing a meal, she notices that Anabel is pretending to do what she does. Anabel sets the table using her toys and she feeds the family. Jack is also joining the game and sits at the table. Anabel places the pretend food in front of Jack and he attempts to throw the food off the plate. Anabel picks up the food and puts it back on Jack's plate. Jack repeats the process by throwing the food at the wall. Brenda walks over to Jack and picks him up and tickles him and says 'What a lovely boy you are, what a clean boy you are'.

Brenda tells Anabel to collect up the food that Jack threw across the room and clean the table. Anabel is angry at having to clean up Jack's food and toys, and asks Brenda to let Jack help. Brenda replies 'Boys don't clear the table – girls do!'

1 What does this incident tell you about the expected gender roles of Jack and Anabel?
2 What was Anabel modelling and what was Brenda reinforcing?
3 How did Brenda show her disapproval at Anabel's request that Jack should help?
4 How were Jack and Anabel's gender roles being learned?

COGNITIVE DEVELOPMENT THEORY

This approach believes that the most important thing in children's gender identity is the level of the child's cognitive development. Children are labelled early in life as boys or girls, and this labelling leads the child to see himself or herself as masculine or feminine. This self-concept of gender, along with the child's growing knowledge of gender, leads the child to organise their way of thinking, whilst exploring activities. For example, a girl might say, 'I am a girl, therefore I am expected (or not expected) to behave in this way'. As the children value aspects of their gender, this approach suggests that they devalue aspects of the other gender.

The child development researcher, Kohlberg, sees the child as active, and the growing awareness of gender identity is significant in how the child's gender role develops. The child observes and imitates role models.

In a number of studies, children's ability to select pictures of men and women and gender self-categorisation has been found to relate to those who spent a lot of time playing with specific gender toys.

Differences between the social learning and cognitive approaches
The social learning view suggests that children develop gender-typed behaviour through reinforcement and observational learning, while the cognitive development approach suggests that children first become aware that there are two categories for people (i.e. male and female), and this informs children of the categories within which they fit. Children then observe and imitate others of the same sex in participating in activities that are appropriate to their gender.

For example, this is how the two theories might explain a girl role-playing at cooking:

- Social learning theory would explain her behaviour in terms of imitation of role models. For example, the girl watches the mother cooking and imitates her.
- Cognitive developmental theory would suggest that the child knows she is a girl and therefore participates in activities that are seen as 'appropriate' for girls.

GOOD PRACTICE

- Always critically evaluate theories in child development.
- Make sure that you know how children learn.

Tanya and I are building a railway. She's shown me what to do.

Theories alone cannot explain how children learn gender roles.

Gender socialisation

Socialisation is the process of learning the norms, values and expectations of the society in which you live (see Chapter 1, page 4). **Gender socialisation** is part of this process – the learning of gender roles.

The process of gender socialisation is performed by the family and by agencies such as playgroups, nurseries, schools, peer groups and the media.

PRIMARY SOCIALISATION

The most important institution to teach us values and expectations of our society is the family, in the process of primary socialisation. Gender roles are taught in the first instance in the home, where models of behaviour are reinforced throughout the child's life in the types of toys given to girls and boys, by the language used to refer to boys and girls – 'Don't be a sissy', 'Boys don't cry', 'Only girls do that' – and in activities that boys and girls are encouraged to engage in (for example, boys help their fathers mend the car, while girls help their mothers with the cooking).

SECONDARY SOCIALISATION

Outside the home (in school, for example), differences between boys and girls are often reinforced.

The influence of adults' attitudes

Choices are usually influenced by teachers and carers, whose values and behaviour influences children by the way they talk and behave towards them, either encouraging children towards certain forms of behaviour or discouraging them from others. This reflects the attributes of the children and the advice they receive.

Children learn quickly to respond in the way adults expect them to. If adults' views of children are based on sex stereotypes, this will result in the children being disadvantaged in later life. For example, girls are more likely to be passive and well-behaved at primary age and this may be considered to be desirable for young girls, but the possible consequence is that they will remain passive and assume that their role in society is to be passive.

Education

The generally accepted position is that girls do better than boys in primary school. They learn to read and count sooner than boys. However, beyond the primary age, there is ample evidence that, in the past, many girls begin to under-achieve in maths, science and technology, while boys do better in these subjects. However, this is no longer necessarily the case – girls are now seen to be achieving, while boys are under-achieving.

Studies show that, on the whole, teachers in primary schools interact more with boys than girls, and from the outset, staff attitudes and expectations of girls and boys strongly influence children's development. A more productive approach would be deliberately to encourage both sexes to work and play together and to treat both boys and girls equally.

In some cases, parents choose to send children to single-sex schools. At school, girls and boys are often found pursuing subjects of study appropriate to gender stereotypes – more girls are found to pursue languages and art subjects compared to boys, who prefer science and mathematics. This is particularly significant in the teenage years.

In some families, the education of boys is regarded as more important than that of girls.

The hidden curriculum

The term **hidden curriculum** refers to specific ways in which girls and boys are expected to behave; it encourages some, while discouraging others. Girls learn to see their future in terms of low-level jobs. Teachers pay more attention to boys, who can expect to reach higher academic achievement than girls. Examples include teachers who praise boys more than girls, who select teaching materials that show girls as passive individuals, or who do not encourage girls in science lessons.

Differences of treatment in the pre-school years have been shown to have negative effects on subsequent academic and social development because they foster limited self-perceptions of abilities, thereby jeopardising future career opportunities.

The media

The mass media contributes significantly to the process of gender socialisation. Newspapers and magazines often portray women as beautiful blondes or 'the housewife', yet men are seldom referred to in this way. Often, women's magazines follow a similar pattern, outlining how women can dress beautifully for men. Television and books portray women negatively.

Children are disadvantaged by sex-role stereotyping when it limits the opportunities available to them. If the socialisation process tells boys and girls that they cannot do something simply because of their gender, then they will believe this and behave as if it were true (the self-fulfilling prophecy, see Chapter 1, page 10).

All professional childcare workers and teachers should avoid sex-role stereotyping of young children, and implement anti-sexist practices.

GOOD PRACTICE

- Be aware of the hidden curriculum and its influence on children's lives.
- Be aware of adults' attitudes and influence on children's perception of gender.
- Treat boys and girls equally.

Activity
Conduct an observation of communication in your placement.
a) What words do the children use when referring to what boys can do and girls can do?
b) Record negative gender stereotyping amongst the children, and between the children and adults.
c) What hidden curriculums can you identify that could convey negative gender role perception and expectations of boys and girls?
d) Do the pictures and books in the placement reflect negative gender expectations of boys and girls? How could this influence the children's socialisation process?
e) What changes would you make in the placement to project positive images to boys and girls?

Anti-sexist practice promotes positive behaviour.

Anti-sexist practice

- Adults can help children to learn about social roles by giving them opportunities to play together.
- Provide good role models.
- Provide resources which promote anti-sexist attitudes.
- Have positive expectations of boys *and* girls.
- Do not discriminate on the basis of sex.
- Avoid sex-role stereotyping.
- Avoid using sexist language. Use language positively to promote anti-sexist attitudes.
- Challenge sexist practices.

QUICK CHECK

1 How could sexist practices and language limit boys' and girls' perception of themselves and their abilities?
2 What is good anti-sexist practice when using language?
3 What are the three theories that aim to explain the origins of gender role development? Briefly summarise the main points of each theory.
4 How does gender socialisation take place?
5 Explain the role of the hidden curriculum in gender socialisation.
6 Summarise the main points of anti-sexist practice.

KEY TERMS

You need to know what these words and phrases mean. Look back through the chapter and check that you understand:

gender	observational learning/modelling
gender roles	sex
gender socialisation	sex stereotyping
hidden curriculum	

6 RACE

This chapter covers:
- **What is race?**
- **What is racism?**
- **Legislation**
- **Challenging racism in the early years environment**
- **Anti-racist practices**

We live in a multicultural society – your nursery nursing programme of study and your placement will reflect this. However, not all college populations will. If your college does not provide such a rich tapestry of stimulating and enriching experience, it is even more important that you understand the issues around the provision of a multicultural environment and have an awareness of anti-racist policies and practices.

We live in a multicultural, multiracial society.

What is race?

Human beings are all members of the same species. This means that if a male and female mate, they are likely to produce offspring who are themselves human beings. The idea of **race** is a social definition, a social construction – a race simply means a group of human beings who see themselves, or are seen by others, as different, a distinct, separate group. This idea of race is based mainly on physical appearance. Large numbers of people are grouped together and called a race because they're said to look alike.

Many biologists reject this view of race as unscientific, and some argue that the genetic make-up of all humans is practically the same. The minor variations that do exist are so minuscule that it makes little sense to talk about different races. Scientists believe that we are a long way from a scientific classification of the human species into types of race. Races are simply social definitions of categories of the human race.

We could, in fact, divide the human species into any number of races based on physical appearance. For example, in the UK people with red hair, blue eyes and a pale skin could be classified as a separate race.

Simply because race is a social definition, it does not mean that we should dismiss it as unimportant. People make race important because of our supposed racial differences. People reject, discriminate against and can kill each other on racial grounds. The idea of race is one of the main factors dividing the human species. See 'What is racism?' on page 137.

Activity

As a group, discuss these questions:
a) Why are classifications of races based on physical appearance unscientific? Why do some biologists refute the idea of different races? Why are scientists a long way from classifying races?
b) 'Race is simply a social definition.' What does this mean? Why is the idea of race important even though it is a social definition?
c) Why would a visitor from outer space be amazed and confused at racial conflict on our planet? Explain using examples.

GOOD PRACTICE

- Encourage parents and community groups to participate in the life of your early years group.
- Use a worldwide approach to help children widen their experiences and learning, i.e. introduce them to different things used around the world, such as food eaten in different countries, or clothes worn.

We are all different, but equal.

What is racism?

Attitudes, prejudices and negative stereotypes are formed early in the process of socialisation. Having a negative attitude towards a person, or group of people, can lead to discrimination against them. (Look back at Chapter 1 for definitions of socialisation, stereotypes, prejudice and discrimination.)

Racism is prejudice against, and discrimination of, people based on their perceived race. It is based on the idea that some races have certain inborn characteristics that make them superior to others, or that a certain race has certain characteristics that are undesirable and so it is inferior to other races. The term 'racist' is used to describe someone who holds these beliefs.

For example, Western white people sometimes perceive themselves as superior to and more intelligent than other races. Few, if any, sociologists would support this belief and use history as evidence to disprove it. When Europe was in the Dark Ages, African civilisation flourished. John Goldthorpe describes the world in the year 1600, when China was probably the most progressive nation, with India and Arabia next. This type of evidence strongly suggests that there is no basis to claim that one so-called race is superior to another.

Racism has many forms; it manifests itself in many ways and is based on skin colour coding and power. It prevents people from fulfilling their own potential as a result of their race. Racism creates a hostile environment for people of different ethnic groups and it fails to encourage positive learning. It prevents access to resources, opportunities and life chances and disadvantages the individual who is experiencing racism.

TYPES OF RACISM

Researchers, such as Bromley and Longino in 1972, refer to three forms of racism, each of which interacts with and reinforces the others:

- **individual racism**, which is personal attitudes and behaviour which individuals use to prejudge racial groups negatively
- **institutional racism**, which draws on society's support of prejudice, i.e. institutions use power to exclude groups of people of different races from access to resources and power, and blame those excluded for their predicament
- **cultural racism**, which includes values, beliefs and ideas which endorse the superiority of white culture over other cultures.

Through these processes, racism permeates and becomes endemic (i.e. it spreads) unless individuals take specific steps to confront it, and to understand how interwoven and complicated the processes of racism are.

CHILDREN AND RACISM

There is a notion that young children are not aware of skin colour and that this is not an issue for the pre-school years. However, research experts, such as Milner in 1936 and Maxime in 1983, have challenged this belief by showing that black children and white children as young as three years old attach value to skin colour. They see white skin as 'better' than black. This suggests that children absorb messages from adults about racial stereotyping from a very early age. This can be damaging for black children, and white children are also affected unless the mis-perception of racial superiority is confronted and challenged positively and effectively.

All young children need to be socialised to avoid making stereotypical assumptions which focus on black children negatively, leading to poor expectations of those children. In 1968 research by Rosenthal and Jacobsen showed that where expectations are low, children often perform badly – the self-fulfilling prophecy (see Chapter 1, page 10).

Siraj Blatchford's research in 1994 indicated that name-calling was the most common form of racism, and that it was not only children who behaved in a racist manner – it included staff in the nurseries and primary schools.

In areas where you are working solely with white children, your training needs to bring you into contact with the richness of the multicultural world that belongs to us all. It is vitally important that you are exposed to these issues, so that you can gain the skills to recognise and competently confront and challenge racism effectively and confidently.

Activity

Plan a story that you could use with a group of young children to educate them about race on the theme of 'different but equal'. Include resources to support the children's learning.

GOOD PRACTICE

- Be aware of the meaning of racism.
- Be aware of how racism is present at the individual, institutional and cultural level.
- Always implement equality practices and challenge racism proactively.

Racism should always be challenged for all of us to benefit.

CASE STUDY

You are in charge of a group of children in a nursery, and you witness the following incident, along with other children in the group.

Ashok, Naheed and Ann are playing in the sandpit. They are all aged 3 years 11 months. Naheed takes a jug of sand and pours it over Ann's hand. Ann tells Naheed that her 'mummy says I'm not to play with Pakis because you eat with your hands and your home stinks of curry'. Naheed and Ashok are upset and leave the sandpit. Ann continues playing, oblivious to the others' reactions.

How would you deal with the situation?
1 What would you say to Ashok and Naheed?
2 How would you deal with the whole group?
3 What aspect of the above case study shows racism?
4 Outline a plan of action and discuss your proposal with your supervisor.
5 Assess the effectiveness of your plan of action in dealing with racism and the children's self-esteem.
6 Would you involve parents, and if so, how would you deal with this? Explain your reasons and decisions, outlining the processes you would undergo.

Legislation

In 1976 the Race Relations Act was passed in the UK (see Chapter 2). It has not successfully combated racial inequality; it prevents people discriminating against others, based on racial origins, but it does not prevent people holding negative and discriminating attitudes towards people from other racial and ethnic groups. Laws alone cannot change racism – people are responsible for bringing about changes for the better.

We live in a pluralistic society, and all children have a right to grow up with positive images of themselves. The Race Relations Act defines 'racial grounds' as colour, race, nationality, ethnic or national origins, but it does not include culture or religion. However, the 1989 Children Act does highlight these.

The Race Relations Act refers to:
• direct discrimination – treating or telling someone that they cannot do or have something on the grounds of their race, nationality or colour

- indirect discrimination – rules and regulations that make it impossible for a member of a specific group to conform to them.

CASE STUDY

The Happy Hours Nursery was opened in a multicultural and multiracial inner-city area (and the children in the nursery reflect this). There are, at present, no black members of staff with an expertise in Asian languages. There is a vacancy for a new member of staff, and the manager has placed this advertisement in the local newspaper:

'Happy Hours Nursery requires a black, Asian language-speaking nursery nurse for 37 hours per week.

CV to be sent to the Manager, Mrs Gertrude Johnson, at the address below.'

1 Is the advertisement legal? If not, say why and what aspect of the Race Relations Act it is contravening.
2 Do you think that the manager could have dealt with the situation in a different way to encourage other ethnic minority applicants? If so, suggest what could have been done, and explain why?

CASE STUDY

Rehanah is a qualified nursery nurse. She is a Muslim and always wears kameez (top) and shalwar (trousers). She applies for a job at a private nursery. She attends for an interview and is successful. However, the job offer is conditional, based on the nursery policy that all female members of staff are expected to wear a skirt.

1 What type of discrimination is the nursery operating?
2 How would you deal with the situation?
3 What recommendations would you make to the nursery in relation to their policies and practices, and why?

GOOD PRACTICE

- Provide positive role models for children.
- Be familiar with the language diversity of the children in your workplace.
- Be aware of race relations recommendations that inform equal rights policies.
- Always follow anti-racist practices when working with young children.

- Racism can be covert (hidden); be aware of this and address it in your everyday practices.
- Be familiar with childcare practices in other cultures.

Challenging racism in the early years environment

Some childcare workers often fail to recognise the racism in specific words and attitudes, and do not know how to deal with the obvious racism, or answer factual questions accurately. As a consequence, racism is left unchallenged and ignorance perpetuates.

When issues of racial differences and racism arise, some people may gloss over them by saying 'That's not a nice thing to say', 'Colour doesn't matter', 'They're not like us', or even 'He can't help being what he is'. These are devices often used for avoiding the necessity of dealing with racism and may in themselves be a direct racist response. Even if you have thought about racism, you need practice to deal with the issues it raises. You need to be able to use explanations that children can understand.

You will be expected to challenge and confront racism. This could be offensive racist policies in college, offensive literature, racist magazines, books, badges, leaflets or racist remarks. It could even be attitudes of other staff in your placement. Some racism, as indicated earlier, could be institutionalised, such as not providing for the dietary needs of certain groups.

All placements and colleges should have anti-racist policies, and you should have access to these. Make sure you are familiar with them.

You may find it difficult to challenge racism at first, whether it is from children or adults, and you may need to discuss strategies for dealing with racism with your supervisor and college tutor.

KEY POINT

Racism can be difficult for some people to challenge. The necessary training should be provided in order to give individuals the confidence to challenge it effectively and proactively.

Activities

1 Look at the books in your placement that are being used by children or adults.

Anti-racist practices

Anti-racist practices are practices based on equality, not racism.

Young children will gain positive experiences if they are accepted and valued for who they are. The 1989 Children Act requires that needs arising from children's race, culture, religion and language should be considered by those working with young children.

The aim of these activities is to widen the children's knowledge of race, culture and diversity. Do not forget that people of all races share similarities in culture.

If possible, take the children to visit places in the local community that represent the cultural diversity of the community – for example, a Sikh temple.

LANGUAGE

Language is very important, because children imitate what they hear and see. Always use politically correct written and spoken words – for example, 'coloured' is no longer an acceptable term. Use 'black', or the person's preferred word. Why not ask the person his or her name? Avoid using the word 'black' where it implies something negative (for example, 'blackmail').

Activity

Working with a group of colleagues:
a) Compile a list which contains negative uses of the word 'black'.
b) Select anti-racist words to replace them.
c) Discuss the words you have used to replace the negative ones. How effective and positive do you think your new words are?
d) How can the nursery nurse contribute to a child's anti-racist vocabulary?

GOOD PRACTICE

Make sure you pronounce and spell all children's names correctly and understand the naming systems of different cultures and religions. For example, Begum, Bi Bi and Kaur are not family surnames – they are titles for a female.

Books

Young children who cannot yet read from books are learning about language from the books which adults choose to make available to them.

Books and literary materials should present a world in which all people are portrayed positively, both in words and pictures. For example, books should portray black children in all aspects of life, taking the lead instead of being in the background. Positive images are necessary to develop the understanding of all children whatever their 'race'. Books which present negative stereotypes should be rejected or used as examples of negative value.

Books with bilingual and multilingual texts will help children to understand that there is more than one written language in the world and that all languages can tell stories.

Children who speak several languages feel all the more valued when home languages are acknowledged by adults working in the early years setting. Children with a command of more than one language should not be viewed negatively or as intellectually impaired – they should be viewed positively as a rich resource of learning within the group of children, and also for staff members who do not share this expertise. You could even ask the children to teach you a few words and translate them into English to assist your understanding.

Activities for children

1 a) Make your own books for children by taking photographs of children and adults and asking them to describe themselves in a couple of sentences under their pictures.

   If the group is all 'white', it is useful as a resource to show all children how different everyone is from each other. It is not only black children who have differences in skin colour, hair and face shape. Let the children identify the differences, for example, hair colour, types of hair, freckles, colours of eyes, skin colours, etc.

   b) Make up special statements with the children, on the theme of 'different but equal'. For example:
   - Things special about me.
   - My favourite things.

   c) Discuss with the children the theme of 'different but equal'.

2 This is an activity using a song which you can use to share other languages with the children. The example is in Punjabi, but you could use the song translated into any language that is not English.

   If you are not fluent in Punjabi, you need to learn the correct pronunciation of the words in the song before you use the activity with the children, otherwise you will be giving the children negative messages. Do not forget that 'white' people also speak fluent Punjabi – language is not always synonymous with skin colour.

This activity gives children a chance to see that songs are not only sung in English and that other people sing songs in their own language – not different songs, but songs which are the same as theirs. Children who share other cultures will value this exercise. This approach is 'different but equal'.

Song in Punjabi
Sir, modhá, goddá pear, goddá pear,
Sir, modhá, goddá pear, goddá pear,
Akkh, te kann, te mukh, te nakk,
Sir, modhá, goddá pear, goddá pear.

Song in English
Head, shoulders, knees and toes,
Head, shoulders, knees and toes,
Eyes and ears and mouth and nose,
Head, shoulders, knees and toes.

3 This is an activity using numbers, which you can use to share other languages with the children. The example is in Urdu, but you could use any other language that is not English. It will give children access to other styles of writing as valuable as English that people in society use everyday.

You will need to practise beforehand, so that you pronounce the numbers correctly. Ask someone who is competent in speaking and writing Urdu to help you.

Numbers in Urdu		Numbers in
Spoken:	Written:	English
ek	١	1
dou	٢	2
thn	٣	3
char	٤	4
panj	٥	5
chaj	٦	6
sat	٧	7
ath	٨	8
naw	٩	9
das	١٠	10

a) Introduce the activity to the children in a positive way.
b) Allow the children to practise the writing.
c) Allow the children to pronounce the words and explain the meanings to the children.
d) Discuss with the children:
   - How did they feel about their new language and writing?
   - Did they enjoy the activity?
e) Having done the activity with the children, how would you evaluate your participation in it?
f) How did the children react to this form of speaking and writing numbers?

GOOD PRACTICE

- Use activities that include pictures of the children to help them to know and appreciate the skin colour they have.
- Understand different types of hair care needed for all children.
- Continually evaluate equipment and books for racism. Dolls, pictures, puzzles, music and songs should reflect many cultures.
- Confront racist remarks, whether from children or from adults, whether directed against yourself or others.
- Answer children's questions about race and culture honestly, with explanations appropriate to the children's age.
- Ask for help and advice from your supervisors if you need it.

Are these good examples of authentic dolls?

PLAY EQUIPMENT

Acquire articles from various parts of the world used in daily life and for special occasions, and also pictures of families from around the world.

Children should be helped to see how the items are used, to avoid them seeing it as something 'silly'. A world view should be taken, with the children being helped to see the value and importance of all play materials from a variety of cultures.

Dolls should be authentic. Be aware that some 'black' dolls are actually dolls with 'white' features, whose skins have been stained with a dye, while others even have 'black' faces and 'white' bodies. This will give children very confusing messages.

DRESSING-UP ACTIVITIES

Dressing-up activities are important because they give children the opportunity to explore, through role-play, the way they see other people. It is a rich opportunity for children to explore other cultures positively, and for this reason the dressing-up clothes should offer the child a wide range of choices – dressing up as a person from another culture can be an enjoyable experience.

Everyday clothes, as well as clothes for special occasions, should be available. Children should be helped to see how the clothes are worn, to avoid the risk of them dismissing it as 'silly'.

You could buy children's versions from the dressing-up ranges on sale. Your institution could purchase the entire range, but ensure that

Clothes such as these are available for dressing-up – they represent cultures and countries of origin, not race.

the garments are authentic, and reflective of garments that people wear in everyday life – not just on special occasions.

Activities for children

1 *Making a kimono.* You could make a kimono following the instructions below or you could provide one. Having done so, create a theme for children (and families, if possible) to participate in. Look at the culture that encompasses the kimono – its religion, language, country of origin, home use and special occasions. It is worn in the UK today by children and adults who share this rich heritage.
2 *Clothes people wear.*
   a) Discuss with the children the types of clothes they wear and types of clothes they see other people wearing.
   b) Organise a session on different types of clothes. Get the children to participate by dressing up. Ask the children:
      ● What is special about your clothes today?
      ● What do you like about it?
      ● When would they wear these types of clothes if they belonged to that culture?
      ● Do they have to be black to wear any of these clothes?
      You could choose a garment from any culture you like and dress in it yourself to communicate positive role modelling to the children (see the example of the sari, below).

How to make a kimono

This will make a kimono for an adult. You can cut the pattern down to make a child's.

You will need:
● for the body and sleeves, a piece of material approximately 1.75 m × 1 m wide
● for the binding and sash (obi), strips of contrasting material as follows:
   – front binding: 1 piece 115 mm wide × 2.194 m long
   – sleeve binding: 2 pieces 89 mm wide × 1.144 m long
   – sash: 1 piece 115 mm wide × 2 m long (or shorter if you wish)
   – alternatively, you might like to make a wider sash

To make up the kimono:
Follow the instructions on page 151 and the diagram on page 150.

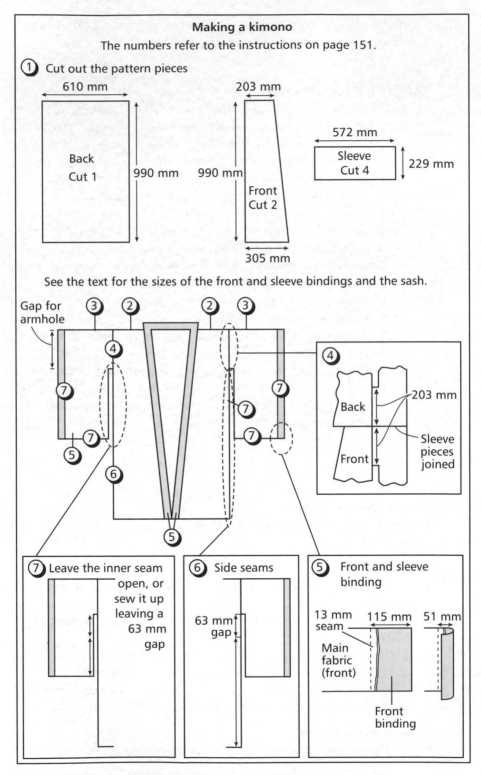

Making a kimono

The numbers refer to the instructions on page 151.

① Cut out the pattern pieces

610 mm

Back
Cut 1

990 mm

203 mm

990 mm

Front
Cut 2

305 mm

572 mm

Sleeve
Cut 4

229 mm

See the text for the sizes of the front and sleeve bindings and the sash.

Gap for armhole

③ ② ② ③

④

⑦ ⑦

⑦ ⑦

⑦

⑤

⑥

⑤

④

Back

Front

203 mm

Sleeve pieces joined

⑦ Leave the inner seam open, or sew it up leaving a 63 mm gap

⑥ Side seams

63 mm gap

⑤ Front and sleeve binding

13 mm seam

115 mm

51 mm

Main fabric (front)

Front binding

Use 13 mm seams throughout.
1 Cut out pieces according to the diagram.
2 Join the front to the back at the shoulders.
3 Join the sleeve pieces together.
4 Join the sleeves to the body with a 406 mm seam across the shoulder seam.
5 Fold the binding strips in half and sew to the kimono. The binding for the front should be 51 mm wide, and the binding for the sleeves should be 38 mm wide.
6 Sew the side seams together, leaving a 63 mm gap below the shoulder seam.
7 Sew the seams around the sleeves together, leaving a gap for the arm-hole at the top. Leave the inner sleeve seam open, or sew it up leaving a 63 mm gap below the shoulder seam.
8 Make the sash. Fold the strip in half lengthways and sew.
9 Finish off all the raw edges.

How to make a sari
You will need:
- a piece of fabric 5.484 m by about 1.143 m wide for an adult. Choose a light-weight material. (Avoid heavy materials because they will not drape well.)
- a blouse
- a long petticoat (waist to toe) with strong elastic in the waist because the sari will be folded into the waistband as you drape it around yourself. You could pin it if you prefer, but this isn't usually the case when worn.
- safe footwear.

If possible, you could take the children to the shop to choose the material – it would be a positive learning experience.

To drape the sari:
The sari is the last thing you put on. Put the blouse and petticoat on first, then the sari. Follow the instructions below and the diagram on page 152. Practise a couple of times before you work with the children. You could choose to drape a sari with the children.
1 Starting at the centre of your back, tuck the sari in at the back of your waist, over your petticoat.
2 Bring the sari around the right hip, across the stomach and round the body to the right hip again. Remember to tuck it into the waist.
3 Make some pleats; they should be identically-sized pleats. Spread out your hands. Each pleat should be the width from your thumb tip to your small finger tip. Fold these in a bunch together and tuck them in at the waist over your right thigh.
4 Wrap the remainder of the sari round your body.
5 Pass it under the right arm.
6 Pass it up and over the chest so it hangs down the back from the left shoulder.

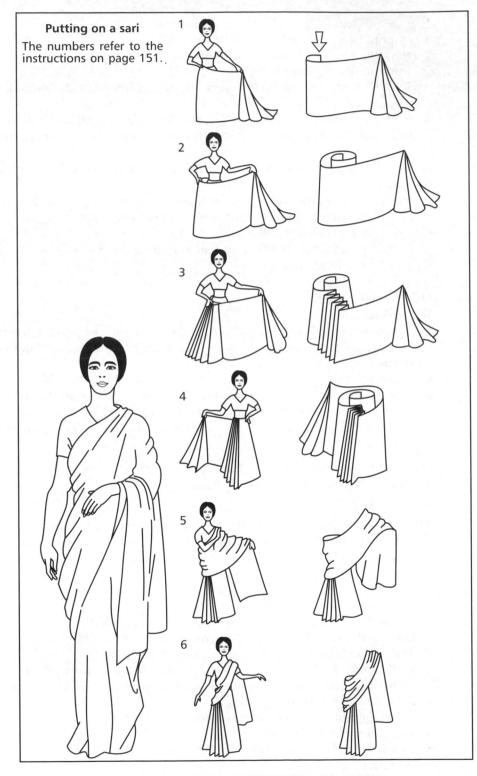

Putting on a sari

The numbers refer to the instructions on page 151. .

1

2

3

4

5

6

GOOD PRACTICE

- Make sure you know and pronounce correctly the names of the garments the children wear, and those they use for dressing up.
- Present positive images of different races in the room, in particular in the book corner and the home corner.
- Present yourself as a good anti-racist role model.
- Acknowledge what you do not know, and be prepared to ask for help and advice.

Activity

On your placement, seek the help of your supervisor with this task.
a) Which religions are represented in the placement?
b) Which major religious or seasonal celebrations and festivals does the placement participate in during the year?
c) Are there any it does not participate in? If not, why?
d) How are the celebrations different from each other in diet, gifts, dress and rituals, if any?

Anti-racist practices should encompass and reflect all children's 'race' and cultural diversity. Language and religion should be portrayed positively in an early years environment. Staff and trainees should participate proactively in producing this rich environment – in the curriculum, in toys, in books, in dietary and religious provisions and in positive role models.

Wherever possible activities should include families and resources from the wider communities.

GOOD PRACTICE

- Develop an understanding that people come from a range of backgrounds and cultures and offer children a secure environment in which to explore their own culture.
- Offer opportunities for children to explore the idea that no culture, language or religion is more superior than others.
- Use pictures and books that depict families from different cultures.
- In wall displays, show people from different ethnic backgrounds doing everyday things.
- Use the children's interests and any knowledge they have of other cultures in planning, and to extend their learning.
- Find appropriate resources and examples from a range of cultures for each topic over and above the everyday multicultural toys, posters, etc.

- Help children talk about and challenge stereotyping.
- Promote children's social and emotional development by recognising the value and importance of their home culture, language, food, religious practices and festivals.
- If there are parents who do not speak English as a first language, make sure that all information is given clearly enough for all the parents to understand. An interpreter may be necessary in some placements.
- Make sure there is a varied menu which will appeal to all children in the nursery, and which will introduce them to a more interesting diet.
- Answer children's questions about racism honestly.
- Seek help and advice if you feel that you have insufficient knowledge and experience about issues of race.
- Always challenge racism.
- Refer to the placement equal opportunities policy on racism. Examine its practices and processes to address issues on racism.
- Be a positive role model for children.
- Always be aware of expectations of professional behaviour and code of practice on placement.

QUICK CHECK

1 How can the socialisation process contribute to young children learning racism?
2 How can we change institutional practices to reduce and combat racism?
3 How could you participate in reducing racism in the early years setting?
4 Outline how you would go about treating black children in the nursery equally.
5 What is direct racial discrimination? Give examples.
6 What is indirect racial discrimination? Give examples.
7 Why should childcare workers challenge racism?
8 How would you ensure that you were confident to do so competently?
9 Summarise the main points of anti-racist practice.

KEY TERMS

You need to know what these words and phrases mean. Look back through the chapter and check that you understand:

anti-racist practice	race
cultural racism	racism
individual racism	worldwide approach
institutional racism	

GLOSSARY

Anti-racist practice Practice based on equality, not racism, which accepts and values people for who they are

Code of practice A set of rules for the practice of particular procedures, either drawn up by individual institutions or as part of legislation

Cultural racism Values, beliefs and ideas which endorse the superiority of white culture over other cultures

Different but equal We are all different, but we are all of equal worth

Direct discrimination Discrimination which is practised overtly (openly), for example refusing a black child a place on the school trip because of his or her colour

Direct racial discrimination Treating or telling someone that they cannot do or have something, on the grounds that they are of another 'race', colour or nationality

Direct sexual discrimination Explicit (overt) statements or acts, based on sex or marital status, which directly affect the treatment of people

Disability A physical or mental impairment which has a substantial and long-term adverse effect on a person's ability to carry out normal, day-to-day activities

Disability discrimination Discrimination on the basis of a person's disability

Disability harassment Harassment based on a person's disability

Disablism Prejudice based on a person's disability

Discrimination Practices which have the effect of putting people of a particular group at a disadvantage

Edu-care Education and caring

Equality of opportunity Providing open access to early childhood services to allow every child and family to participate fully, and treating all children equally, based on their individual needs

Equal opportunities policy A plan of action drawn up by an institution, based on its legal responsibilities under equal rights legislation, outlining how these should be implemented

Gender A label that is socially constructed, it describes the cultural and psychological expectations of behaviour as being either typically male behaviour or typically female behaviour. It is a product of socialisation. Dress is also a part of this

Gender roles Behaviour that is regarded as appropriate for one gender and inappropriate for the other

Gender socialisation The learning of gender roles from one's family, playgroups, nurseries, school, peer groups, the media, etc.

Good practice The promotion of equal opportunities, which is achieved by implementing anti-discriminating practices, i.e. putting equal opportunities into action

Harassment A form of direct discrimination. To harass someone means to trouble or torment them with persistent 'attacks'

Hidden curriculum Specific, 'hidden' ways in which schools expect girls and boys to behave, usually apparent in the way girls and boys are treated in school; it encourages some, while discouraging others

Impairment An inability to do something – to be unable to walk is an impairment, whereas disability is the lack of provision and facilities, such as lifts and ramps, which could provide mobility

Inclusive approach Including all children in a nursery in activities, not excluding any on the grounds of disability

Indirect discrimination Discrimination which favours one group over another. It mainly takes the form of practices that are covert (hidden) – rules and regulations that make it impossible for a person belonging to a specific group to participate fully in society

Indirect racial discrimination Treatment which may be described as equal in a formal sense, but which is discriminatory in its effects on one particular racial group, and which occurs when regulations or rules are put into practice which are impossible for that racial group to conform to

Indirect sexual discrimination Covert (hidden) practices, such as regulations, which are not applied equally to men and women, or to married and single people. This has the effect of disadvantaging a very high proportion of the population

Individual education plan At Stage 2 of the assessment process for special education needs, this plan sets out the action to be taken and targets to be achieved

Individual racism Personal attitudes and behaviour which individuals use to prejudge racial groups negatively

Institutional racism Racism which draws on society's support of prejudice, i.e. institutions use power to exclude groups of people of different races from access to resources and power, and blame those excluded for their predicament

Intentional harassment An offence created by Section 154 of the 1994 Criminal Justice and Public Order Act, of 'intentionally causing harassment, alarm or distress through using threatening behaviour or displays'

Modelling *See* Observational learning

Negative stereotyping An inaccurate stereotype which ignores individual differences among people

Observational learning Part of social learning theory: children's behaviour is shaped by the behaviour of others – they learn gender differences in behaviour and attitudes by observation, imitation and reinforcement (reward or disapproval). Also known as *modelling*

Positive action For example, providing access to training for a particular ethnic group when during the past twelve months, no (or very few) members of that ethnic group have been undertaking particular work, or encouraging members of an ethnic group to take advantage of opportunities for doing a particular kind of work

Prejudice Literally means prejudgement. It results from a person's (or a group's) failure to explore alternative explanations or possibilities for their stereotypes

Primary socialisation Socialisation which usually occurs in the home with family and close friends

Principles of good practice Knowledge of equal rights legislation, your responsibilities under that legislation, and putting them into practice; knowledge of the the organisation's equal opportunities policy and codes of practice and your responsibilities, and putting them into practice; knowledge of anti-discriminatory practices and their implementation; using language and resources in the early years setting which promote equal opportunities; on-going training in equal opportunities practices; taking part in regular staff development, appraisal and review sessions to maintain standards of good practice

Race A label that is socially constructed, it describes a group of people who see themselves, or who are seen by others, to have the same ethnic origin. It is often an assumption based on a person's outward appearance and skin colour

Racial discrimination Discrimination on the basis of a person's 'race'. The Race Relations Act defines discrimination as: 'On racial grounds, "he" treats that other person less favourably than "he" treats or would treat other persons.' ['He' includes 'she' for the purposes of the Act.] The Act defines 'racial grounds' as colour, race, nationality, ethnic or national origins. It does not include culture or religion

Racial harassment Derogatory remarks, racially explicit statements that are negative; graffiti, jokes, or any action of a racist nature which is directed at an individual or group from a different ethnic background and which results in the individual(s) feeling threatened or compromised

Racism Prejudice based on a person's race

Scapegoating To project the blame for something on to others, instead of looking at the real causes

Secondary socialisation Socialisation which includes other agencies, such as playgroups, childminders, schools, etc.

Segregation Setting someone (or a group) apart from another on the basis of their race

Self-actualisation Achieving one's full potential

Self-esteem Respect for oneself and having the respect (esteem) of others

Self-fulfilling prophecy A process of conditioning people to behave in ways based on other people's expectations of them

Sex A biological term, it refers to the biological differences between males and females. Sex is usually unchanging, but can be changed by surgery

Sexism Prejudice based on a person's biological sex

Sexual discrimination Discrimination on the basis of a person's sex

Sexual harassment Any harassing conduct based on the gender of the recipient. The European Commission Code of Conduct defines it as: 'Unwanted conduct of a sexual nature based on sex, affecting the dignity of women and men at work'

Sex stereotyping An assumption about a person based on their sex

Socialisation The process of learning the norms, values and expectations of the society in which you live, including language, gender behaviour, culture and religion

Special educational needs Special needs (see below), which relate to a child's education

Special needs A term used in childcare settings to describe children that are different but equal – children with special needs are those who do not follow the general pattern of developmental stages, for a number of reasons. Special needs may be physical conditions, related to language and speech, sensory impairments, learning difficulties, emotional and behavioural difficulties, gifted children

Statementing Stage 5 of the assessment process, in which a document (a 'statement') is drawn up, which states a child's particular educational needs and how the local educational authority will meet those needs with support, which may be in a mainstream school or special provision

Statutory assessment Stage 4 of the assessment process, in which documentary evidence is collected to demonstrate that, despite the steps taken through Stages 1–3, a child's educational needs remain so great that they cannot be provided from resources 'ordinarily available'

Stereotype/stereotyping A mental structure which contains an individual

Tokenistic behaviour Pretending to value something when in fact you don't, also described as 'lip service'

Victimisation Imposing sanctions on a person (or a group) on the basis of their race

Worldwide approach To help children widen their experiences and learn about other cultures, introduce them to different things used around the world, such as food eaten in different countries, or clothes worn

Useful addresses

Coeliac UK, PO Box 220, High Wycombe, Bucks HP11 2HY

Cystic Fibrosis Trust, 11 London Road, Bromley, Kent BR1 1BY

Diabetes UK, 10 Parkway, London NW1 17AA

Down's Syndrome Association, 155 Mitcham Road, London SW17 9PG

Epilepsy Action, New Anstey House, Gateway Drive, Yeadon, Leeds LS19 7XY

Equal Opportunities Commission (EOC), Overseas House, Quay Street, Manchester M3 3HN (0161 833 9244)

HIV and AIDS, Terence Higgins Trust, 52–54 Gray's Inn Road, London WC1X 8JU

Hyperactive Children's Support Group, 71 Whyke Lane, Chichester, West Sussex PO19 7PD

National Association for Giften Children, Suite 14, Challenge House, Sherwood Drive, Bletchley, Milton Keynes MK3 6DP

National Asthma Campaign, Providence House, Providence Place, London NW1 0NT

National Autistic Association, 393 City Road, London EC1V 1NG

Save the Children, Equality Learning Centre, The Resource Centre, 356 Holloway Road, London N7 6PA (0171 700 8127)

SCOPE, 6 Market Road, London, N7 9PW

Sickle Cell Society, 54 Station Road, Harlesden, London NW10 4UA

Working Group Against Racism in Children's Resources, 460 Wandsworth Road, London SW8 3LX (0171 627 4594)

FURTHER READING

Bainbridge, C. (1995) Trying to find the right words, *Everywoman*, May

Bastiani, J. (1989) *Working With Parents: A Whole School Approach*, NFER-Nelson

British Psychological Society (1988) Guidelines for the use of non-sexist language, *The Psychologist*, February

Code of Practice for Schools 2002

Disability Discrimination Act 1995, Part 4

Disability Rights Commission 2002, UK Stationery Office

Dixon, B. (1977) *Catching Them Young*, Trentham Books

Dixon, B. (1990) *Playing Them False*, Trentham Books

DoH & Home Office (1991) *Working Together Under the Children Act 1989*, HMSO

Hales, G. (ed.) *Beyond Disability: Towards An Enabling Society*, Sage

Laishley, J. (1987) *Working With Young Children*, Hodder & Stoughton

Lindon, J. and Lindon, I. (1993) *Caring For The Under 8s*, Macmillan

Moore, S. (1996) *Sociology Alive!*, 2nd edition, Stanley Thornes

SEN Toolkit, DfES Publications

Special Educational Needs Code of Practice, November 2001, DfES Publications

Stainton Rogers, W. and Roche, J. (1994) *Children's Welfare and Children's Rights: A Practical Guide to the Law*, Hodder & Stoughton

White, P. (1995) *Playing Fair: A Parents' Guide to Tackling Discrimination*, UK edition, National Early Years Network/Save the Children

Equal Chances (1991, revised 1996), Pre-school Learning Alliance

The Best Of Both Worlds: Celebrating Mixed Parentage, Early Years Trainers Anti-Racist Network

INDEX